MW00593288

Great
Intentions

A Collection of Recipes from the Endoscopy Center at Robinwood

Great Intentions

A Collection of Recipes from the Endoscopy Center at Robinwood

Published by
The Endoscopy Center at Robinwood
11110 Medical Campus Road, Suite 248
Hagerstown, Maryland 21742

Copyright © 2008 by
The Endoscopy Center at Robinwood

Cover Photography Copyright © by Brian Moyer
Cover Concept by Brian and Nancy Moyer

This cookbook is a collection of favorite recipes, which are not necessarily original recipes.

ISBN: 978-0-9789256-5-9

Edited, Designed, and Produced by
CommunityClassics™

An imprint of
FRP
P. O. Box 305142
Nashville, Tennessee 37230
800-358-0560

Manufactured in China
First Printing: 2008
3,000 copies

Dedication

With gratitude to our patients.
May all your days be filled with good health
and the magic of love.

The Blue Star Symbol for colorectal cancer consists of a blue
ribbon merged with a blue star, assuming a human
shape. It represents the eternal memory of those who lost
their lives to colorectal cancer and the shining hope for
a future free of colon cancer.

Acknowledgments

The Staff of the Endoscopy Center at Robinwood wishes to
express its gratitude to all who have graciously contributed to the
successful publication of **Great Intentions**. The support and assistance
from the staff of Digestive Disorders Consultants, Gastroenterology
Associates, and The Robinwood Department of Anesthesia is sincerely
appreciated. A special thank you to those who have so
enthusiastically shared their favorite family and gourmet recipes.

The nutritional analysis is the result of many hours of dedication
by *Karen Cremins*, RD.

The front and back covers were designed by *Brian Moyer*, CRNA,
Robinwood Department of Anesthesia, and *Nancy Moyer*.

The name *Great Intentions* was created by *Penny Nicarry*,
Manager of the Endoscopy Center at Robinwood.

A special thank you to Salix Pharmaceuticals, Inc.,
Maureen Zimmerman, Territory Manager for contributing to
the success of this cookbook with a generous donation.

Table of Contents

Introduction

We all want to eat healthfully—most of the time. With an abundance of tempting food, not all low in fat and high in fiber, it is challenging to eat nutritiously at every meal. Perhaps a more realistic goal involves balance—ensuring that most of our diet is nutritious while allowing some occasional delicious indiscretions.

It is the Great Intention of the contributors of this cookbook to provide the nutritional information necessary to help you achieve a dietary balance. A proper diet and exercise can decrease your risk of developing heart disease, diabetes, and cancer. A proper diet can also improve the symptoms from gastrointestinal disorders such as Crohn's disease, ulcerative colitis, irritable bowel syndrome, and celiac disease. However, before these conditions can be treated a diagnosis must be determined. This is when we, the Endoscopy Center at Robinwood, enter the picture.

The Endoscopy Center at Robinwood is a freestanding outpatient medical facility specializing in the diagnosis of gastrointestinal disorders. Since opening in the fall of 2002, our gastroenterologists have performed approximately 7,000 colonoscopies and upper gastrointestinal endoscopy procedures annually. Having provided care to more than 33,000 patients, the staff has become acutely aware of the need for improved patient education as well as the importance of medical research.

The adult gastrointestinal tract is twenty-six feet in length and may contain many types of pathology. Through early diagnosis and treatment, most diseases are preventable, curable, or at the very least, controllable. It is especially well documented that when colon cancer is detected early, 90 percent of those patients have at least a five-year survival rate. The American College of Gastroenterology has established guidelines recommending when to have a colonoscopy or esophago-gastroduodenscopy (EGD). Your doctor is familiar with these guidelines.

The contributors to this cookbook want to beat colon cancer or at the very least, remove it from being the second most common cause of cancer deaths among Americans. To support this goal, the staff members of the Endoscopy Center at Robinwood, Digestive Disorders Consultants, Gastroenterology Associates, and Robinwood Department of Anesthesia have published this cookbook. All profits will be donated to charity and to the continued research of gastrointestinal disorders.

To you—our patients, family and friends—it is our Great Intention that this cookbook will serve as a miniature reference book as well as a cookbook. We have included educational information about the more common GI disorders as well as nutritional information for each of our favorite recipes.

Thank you for purchasing this cookbook, thereby contributing to improving the treatment of gastrointestinal disorders.

The Staff of the Endoscopy Center at Robinwood

Nutritional Profile Guidelines

The nutritional analysis which accompanies each of the recipes is to serve **only** as a guideline. If a medical condition or illness requires close dietary monitoring, **please** consult your physician or a registered dietician.

When computing the nutritional analysis, the following standards were used for specific ingredients. The analysis is for the specified serving size.

1. Artificial sweeteners were not substituted for sugar.
2. Alcohol was analyzed.
3. Dry cake mix was analyzed along with the other ingredients in the recipe.
4. All eggs used were considered large.
5. All flour was analyzed as unsifted all-purpose flour, unless stated differently.
6. Butter and margarine were regular, not softened or whipped.
7. All cream cheese was analyzed as regular, unless stated as 1/3-less-fat, low-fat, or fat-free.
8. Milk was 2 percent. Buttermilk was 2 percent. Evaporated milk was 4 percent.
9. Oil used was vegetable oil.
10. Salt to taste, extracts, marinades, and garnishes were not analyzed.
11. If a range of an ingredient amount was given, the larger amount was analyzed.
12. The "grease and flour" ingredients used in pan preparation were not analyzed.

Appetizers & Beverages

Preventive Medicine

Preventive medicine is important and ultimately saves lives and health care dollars. Among deaths caused by cancer, colon cancer is the second-leading killer of Americans, second only to lung cancer in lethality. It is, however, a preventable disease. For cancer prevention, when should an individual have a "Gut Check"? For patients with no family history of colon cancer, a colonoscopy should first be performed at age fifty. If the examination is normal, then it should be repeated at ten-year intervals. For those who have a first-degree relative (mother, father, brother, sister) with a history of colon cancer, a colonoscopy should be performed at age forty. A colonoscopy allows for identification of polyps (small growths that can eventually grow into cancer) and their subsequent removal. A polypectomy, or removal of a polyp, is a necessary step for cancer prevention. Remember, by having a colonoscopy, the life you save may be your own.

Charlie Brown's Peanut Butter Triangles

2 tablespoons peanut butter
2 slices white bread, crusts removed
1 tablespoon grape jelly

Spread the peanut butter evenly on one side of each bread slice, spreading to the edges. Spread the jelly over the peanut butter on one slice and top with the remaining bread slice, peanut butter side down. Slice the sandwich diagonally from corner to corner to form four triangles. Enjoy.

Yield: 1 serving

 Nutrients Per Serving: Cal 389; Cal from Fat 164; T Fat 18.3 g; Saturated Fat 3.7 g; 42.2% Cal from Fat; Chol 0 mg; Sod 425 mg; T Carbo 44 g; 45.3% Cal from Carbo; Fiber 3 g; Prot 12.2 g; 12.6% Cal from Prot

CHARLIE BROWN PREFERS WHITE BREAD, BUT JEAN SCHULZ SUGGESTS USING A DELICIOUS ARTISAN BREAD FROM A BAKERY SUCH AS WILDFLOWER BREAD IN FREESTONE, CALIFORNIA. CHARLIE BROWN IS A TRADEMARK OF UNITED FEATURE SYNDICATE, INC. ALL RIGHTS RESERVED.

Creamy Herbed Spinach Dip

1 (10-ounce) package frozen chopped
    spinach, thawed and drained
1/2 cup sour cream
1/2 cup mayonnaise
1/2 cup packed flat-leaf parsley
2 ounces feta cheese, crumbled
2 tablespoons thinly sliced
    scallion bulbs

1 tablespoon chopped fresh dill weed
1 tablespoon lemon juice
1 teaspoon grated lemon zest
1 small garlic clove, minced or
    pressed (about 1 teaspoon)
1/4 teaspoon pepper
Salt to taste

Press the excess moisture from the spinach. Combine the spinach, sour cream, mayonnaise, parsley, cheese, scallions, dill weed, lemon juice, lemon zest, garlic and pepper in a food processor. Process for 30 seconds or until smooth and creamy. Taste and season with salt. Serve with vegetable crudités and pita chips or assorted party crackers.

Yield: 24 servings

Nutrients Per Serving: Cal 51; Cal from Fat 44; T Fat 4.8 g; Saturated Fat 1.5 g; 85.9% Cal from Fat; Chol 6 mg; Sod 69 mg; T Carbo 1 g; 7.8% Cal from Carbo; Fiber 0.4 g; Prot 0.8 g; 6.2% Cal from Prot

> FOODS THAT ARE HIGH IN BETA-CAROTENE MAY SUPPRESS THE PROCESS OF
> CANCER WITHIN THE CELL. GOOD SOURCES OF BETA-CAROTENE ARE SWEET POTATOES,
> CARROTS, SPINACH, CANTALOUPES, BROCCOLI, AND ROMAINE.

Spinach Artichoke Dip

1 (10-ounce) package frozen spinach,
    thawed and drained
12 ounces cream cheese, softened
2 (4-ounce) jars marinated artichoke
    hearts, drained and chopped
1/2 cup mayonnaise

2 tablespoons grated
    Parmesan cheese
3 garlic cloves, chopped
1/8 teaspoon Tabasco sauce
1 1/2 cups dry bread crumbs

Press the excess moisture from the spinach. Combine the spinach, cream cheese, artichokes, mayonnaise, Parmesan cheese, garlic and Tabasco sauce in a bowl and mix until combined.

Spoon into a 7×11-inch baking dish and sprinkle with the bread crumbs. Bake at 375 degrees for 25 minutes.

Yield: 24 servings

Nutrients Per Serving: Cal 122; Cal from Fat 85; T Fat 9.6 g; Saturated Fat 3.8 g; 69.6% Cal from Fat; Chol 18 mg; Sod 189 mg; T Carbo 6.9 g; 22.6% Cal from Carbo; Fiber 0.5 g; Prot 2.4 g; 7.9% Cal from Prot

Nacho Dip

8 ounces cream cheese, softened
1 (15-ounce) can chili without beans
2 cups (8 ounces) shredded Cheddar cheese

Spread the cream cheese over the bottom of a microwave-safe pie plate. Spread the chili over the cream cheese and sprinkle with the Cheddar cheese. Microwave for 5 minutes or until the cheese melts.

Yield: 16 servings

Nutrients Per Serving: Cal 129; Cal from Fat 93; T Fat 10.3 g; Saturated Fat 6.3 g; 71.9% Cal from Fat; Chol 35 mg; Sod 239 mg; T Carbo 2.6 g; 8% Cal from Carbo; Fiber 0.3 g; Prot 6.5 g; 20.1% Cal from Prot

Seven-Layer Taco Dip

1 (16-ounce) can jalapeño bean dip
1 (16-ounce) container avocado dip
1/2 cup mayonnaise
1/2 cup sour cream
1/2 envelope taco seasoning mix
1 1/2 to 2 cups (6 to 8 ounces) shredded Cheddar cheese
1 (2-ounce) can sliced black olives, drained
2 tomatoes, chopped
1 bunch green onions with tops, chopped

Spread the bean dip over the bottom of a 10-inch pie plate. Spread the avocado dip over the bean dip. Combine the mayonnaise, sour cream and taco seasoning mix in a bowl and spread over the prepared layers. Sprinkle with the cheese, olives, tomatoes and green onions. Serve with corn chips or your favorite chips.

Yield: 16 servings

 Nutrients Per Serving: Cal 248; Cal from Fat 192; T Fat 21.4 g; Saturated Fat 7.2 g; 77.3% Cal from Fat; Chol 25 mg; Sod 569 mg; T Carbo 7.5 g; 12.1% Cal from Carbo; Fiber 1.2 g; Prot 6.6 g; 10.6% Cal from Prot

Hot Crab Dip

16 ounces light cream cheese, softened
1/2 cup minced fresh parsley
1/2 cup reduced-fat sour cream
1/4 cup mayonnaise
2 tablespoons white wine or sherry
2 tablespoons grated onion
1 tablespoon Dijon mustard
1 teaspoon chopped garlic
4 dashes of Tabasco sauce
1 pound crab meat, drained and flaked
1/2 cup slivered almonds
Paprika to taste

Mix the cream cheese, parsley, sour cream, mayonnaise, wine, onion, Dijon mustard, garlic and Tabasco sauce in a bowl. Add the crab meat and mix gently until combined. Spoon into a baking dish and sprinkle with the almonds and paprika.

Bake, covered with foil, at 325 degrees for 20 minutes. Remove the foil and broil for 2 minutes or until the almonds are brown. Serve warm with assorted party crackers and/or crusty French bread. Freeze for future use, if desired.

Yield: 48 servings

Nutrients Per Serving: Cal 53; Cal from Fat 37; T Fat 3.8 g; Saturated Fat 1.4 g; 70.3% Cal from Fat; Chol 13 mg; Sod 84 mg; T Carbo 1.1 g; 8.4% Cal from Carbo; Fiber 0.2 g; Prot 2.8 g; 21.3% Cal from Prot

Crab Dip with Old Bay

16 ounces cream cheese, softened
1 cup sour cream
3 tablespoons mayonnaise
1 pound crab meat, drained and flaked
1 tablespoon Worcestershire sauce
1/4 teaspoon garlic salt
Old Bay seasoning to taste
1 cup (4 ounces) shredded Cheddar cheese

Combine the cream cheese, sour cream and mayonnaise in a bowl and mix until blended. Add the crab meat, Worcestershire sauce, garlic salt and Old Bay seasoning and mix gently until combined.

Spoon into an 8×8-inch baking dish and sprinkle with the Cheddar cheese. Bake at 350 degrees for 30 to 35 minutes or until heated through. Serve with assorted party crackers, bread rounds and/or celery sticks.

Yield: 96 servings

Nutrients Per Serving: Cal 35; Cal from Fat 27; T Fat 2.9 g; Saturated Fat 1.5 g; 78% Cal from Fat; Chol 11 mg; Sod 46 mg; T Carbo 0.2 g; 2.3% Cal from Carbo; Fiber 0 g; Prot 1.7 g; 19.7% Cal from Prot

Crab and Artichoke Dip

Baked Pita Chips
7 pita bread rounds

Dip
8 ounces cream cheese,
   softened
1 cup mayonnaise
1 garlic clove, pressed
1 (14-ounce) can artichoke hearts,
   drained and chopped

8 ounces fresh crab meat, drained
   and flaked
$3/4$ cup (3 ounces) freshly grated
   Parmesan cheese
$1/3$ cup thinly sliced green onions
   with tops
1 teaspoon grated lemon zest
$1/8$ teaspoon pepper
$1/3$ cup chopped red bell pepper
Sliced green onions for garnish

To prepare the chips, cut each pita round horizontally into halves. Cut each half into eight wedges. Arrange the wedges in a single layer on a flat baking stone. Bake at 400 degrees for 8 to 10 minutes or until light brown. Remove to a wire rack to cool. Store in an airtight container.

To prepare the dip, mix the cream cheese, mayonnaise and garlic in a bowl until combined. Combine the artichokes, crab meat, Parmesan cheese, $1/3$ cup green onions, the lemon zest and pepper in a bowl and mix well. Add to the cream cheese mixture and mix well.

Spoon into a deep baking dish and bake at 350 degrees for 25 to 30 minutes or until brown around the edges. Sprinkle with the bell pepper and sliced green onions. Serve warm with the chips.

Yield: 16 servings

Nutrients Per Serving: Cal 255; Cal from Fat 151; T Fat 16.8 g; Saturated Fat 5.5 g; 59.1% Cal from Fat; Chol 36 mg; Sod 473 mg; T Carbo 17.5 g; 27.4% Cal from Carbo; Fiber 1.2 g; Prot 8.6 g; 13.5% Cal from Prot

Cheesy Crab Dip

8 ounces extra sharp Cheddar
    cheese, chopped
8 ounces sliced sharp American
    cheese, chopped
5 ounces sharp white Cheddar
    cheese, chopped

$^1/_3$ cup milk
$^1/_4$ cup dry white wine
1 (16-ounce) can crab meat, drained
    and flaked

Combine the extra sharp Cheddar cheese, American cheese and white Cheddar cheese in a saucepan. Cook over low heat until the cheese melts, adding the milk gradually and stirring constantly.

Stir the wine and crab meat into the cheese mixture and cook until heated through. Spoon into a chafing dish and serve with toasted onion bagels.

Yield: 24 servings

Nutrients Per Serving: Cal 119; Cal from Fat 76; T Fat 8.4 g; Saturated Fat 5.1 g; 63.8% Cal from Fat; Chol 42 mg; Sod 296 mg; T Carbo 0.8 g; 2.7% Cal from Carbo; Fiber 0 g; Prot 10 g; 33.6% Cal from Prot

Shrimp Dip

8 ounces cream cheese, softened
$^1/_2$ cup mayonnaise-style
    salad dressing
$^1/_3$ cup chopped red onion

1 (4-ounce) can tiny shrimp, drained
    and rinsed
$^1/_8$ teaspoon garlic salt

Mix the cream cheese and salad dressing in a bowl until blended. Stir in the onion, shrimp and garlic salt. Chill, covered, until serving time. Serve with assorted party crackers.

Yield: 24 servings

Nutrients Per Serving: Cal 60; Cal from Fat 46; T Fat 5 g; Saturated Fat 2.3 g; 76.7% Cal from Fat; Chol 19 mg; Sod 81 mg; T Carbo 1.7 g; 11.3% Cal from Carbo; Fiber 0 g; Prot 1.8 g; 12% Cal from Prot

Spicy Shrimp Dip

8 ounces cream cheese, softened
1/2 cup mayonnaise
3 to 4 tablespoons lemon juice
3 tablespoons ketchup
1 teaspoon prepared horseradish
1/2 teaspoon onion salt
1/4 teaspoon Worcestershire sauce
10 drops of Tabasco sauce
2 (5-ounce) cans tiny shrimp, drained

Combine the cream cheese, mayonnaise, lemon juice, ketchup, horseradish, onion salt, Worcestershire sauce and Tabasco sauce in a bowl and mix well. Stir in the shrimp. Chill, covered, for 2 hours or longer. Serve with assorted chips and/or party crackers.

Note: The flavor is enhanced if chilled for 8 to 10 hours.

Yield: 16 servings

Nutrients Per Serving: Cal 120; Cal from Fat 92; T Fat 10.2 g; Saturated Fat 4 g; 76.9% Cal from Fat; Chol 49 mg; Sod 153 mg; T Carbo 1.7 g; 5.7% Cal from Carbo; Fiber 0 g; Prot 5.2 g; 17.4% Cal from Prot

Shrimp Salad Salsa

2¹/2 pounds shrimp, cooked, peeled
    and chopped
1 (24-ounce) jar mild salsa
2 cups chopped fresh cilantro

2 cups chopped tomatoes
¹/2 cup chopped red onion
2 tablespoons lime juice

Combine the shrimp, salsa, cilantro, tomatoes, onion and lime juice in a bowl and mix well. Chill, covered, for 8 to 10 hours, stirring occasionally. Serve with tortilla chips.

Yield: 48 servings

Nutrients Per Serving: Cal 27; Cal from Fat 2; T Fat 0.3 g; Saturated Fat 0.1 g; 7.4% Cal from Fat; Chol 46 mg; Sod 129 mg; T Carbo 1.2 g; 17.6% Cal from Carbo; Fiber 0.3 g; Prot 5.1 g; 75% Cal from Prot

Cheese Spread

8 ounces cold pack sharp
    Cheddar cheese
8 ounces cream cheese, softened
2 tablespoons margarine, softened
2 tablespoons chopped onion

2 tablespoons chopped green
    bell pepper
2 tablespoons chopped pimento
1 teaspoon Worcestershire sauce
¹/2 teaspoon lemon juice

Combine the Cheddar cheese, cream cheese and margarine in a bowl and mix until blended. Stir in the onion, bell pepper, pimento, Worcestershire sauce and lemon juice. Chill, covered, until serving time. Serve with assorted party crackers, celery sticks and/or melba toast rounds.

Yield: 32 servings

Nutrients Per Serving: Cal 52; Cal from Fat 42; T Fat 4.7 g; Saturated Fat 2.6 g; 80.2% Cal from Fat; Chol 12 mg; Sod 126 mg; T Carbo 0.9 g; 6.9% Cal from Carbo; Fiber 0 g; Prot 1.7 g; 13% Cal from Prot

Salmon Party Ball

1 (16-ounce) can salmon, drained and flaked
8 ounces cream cheese, softened
1 tablespoon lemon juice
2 teaspoons grated onion
1 teaspoon prepared horseradish
1/4 teaspoon salt
1/4 teaspoon liquid smoke
1/4 cup chopped pecans
3 tablespoons parsley

Combine the salmon, cream cheese, lemon juice, onion, horseradish, salt and liquid smoke in a bowl and mix well. Chill, covered, for several hours.

Shape into a ball and coat with the pecans and parsley. Chill, covered, until serving time. Serve with assorted party crackers.

Yield: 24 servings

Nutrients Per Serving: Cal 67; Cal from Fat 47; T Fat 5.2 g; Saturated Fat 2.5 g; 69.7% Cal from Fat; Chol 20 mg; Sod 159 mg; T Carbo 0.6 g; 3.6% Cal from Carbo; Fiber 0.1 g; Prot 4.5 g; 26.7% Cal from Prot

Tuna Mousse

2 envelopes unflavored gelatin
1/4 cup cold water
2 (6-ounce) cans water-pack tuna, drained
1 (10-ounce) can cream of mushroom soup
8 ounces cream cheese, cubed and softened
1 cup mayonnaise
1 small onion, chopped
1 teaspoon mayonnaise

Dissolve the gelatin in the water in a measuring cup. Combine the tuna, soup and cream cheese in a saucepan and cook over low heat until heated through, stirring occasionally. Stir in the gelatin mixture, 1 cup mayonnaise and the onion.

Coat an 8-inch mold with 1 teaspoon mayonnaise and spoon the tuna mixture into the prepared mold. Chill, covered, in the refrigerator until set. Invert the mousse onto a serving platter and serve with assorted party crackers.

Yield: 24 servings

Nutrients Per Serving: Cal 127; Cal from Fat 100; T Fat 11.1 g; Saturated Fat 3.3 g; 78.9% Cal from Fat; Chol 17 mg; Sod 178 mg; T Carbo 1.5 g; 4.7% Cal from Carbo; Fiber 0.1 g; Prot 5.2 g; 16.4% Cal from Prot

Marvelous Marinated Mushrooms

3 pounds button mushrooms, stems removed
1 teaspoon salt
1¹/2 cups vegetable oil
¹/3 cup fresh lemon juice
1 envelope garlic salad dressing mix
2 tablespoons parsley flakes
2 tablespoons garlic powder
Salt and pepper to taste

Combine the mushroom caps and 1 teaspoon salt with enough water to cover in a saucepan and bring to a boil. Boil for 1 minute; drain.

Mix the oil, lemon juice, salad dressing mix, parsley flakes, garlic powder, salt and pepper in a bowl and mix well. Pour over the mushroom caps in a shallow dish and turn to coat. Marinate, covered, in the refrigerator for 24 hours or longer, turning occasionally. Drain and serve chilled.

Yield: 6 servings

Nutrients Per Serving: Cal 587; Cal from Fat 499; T Fat 55.5 g; Saturated Fat 7 g; 85% Cal from Fat; Chol 0 mg; Sod 765 mg; T Carbo 16.6 g; 11.3% Cal from Carbo; Fiber 3.2 g; Prot 5.4 g; 3.7% Cal from Prot

Spinach Balls

2 (10-ounce) packages frozen chopped spinach,
    thawed and drained
3 cups dry stuffing mix
1 large onion, finely chopped (about 1 cup)
3/4 cup (1 1/2 sticks) margarine, melted
1/2 cup (2 ounces) finely grated Parmesan cheese
6 eggs, beaten
1 teaspoon garlic salt
1 teaspoon pepper

Press the excess moisture from the spinach. Combine the spinach, stuffing mix, onion, margarine, cheese, eggs, garlic salt and pepper in a bowl and mix well. Shape into balls the size of a rounded teaspoon.

Arrange the spinach balls in a single layer in a 9×13-inch baking pan. Bake at 350 degrees for 15 to 20 minutes or until heated through. Serve immediately.

Note: Freeze for future use and reheat in a conventional oven or in the microwave.

Yield: 12 servings

Nutrients Per Serving: Cal 285; Cal from Fat 145; T Fat 16.3 g; Saturated Fat 3.8 g; 50.9% Cal from Fat; Chol 108 mg; Sod 743 mg; T Carbo 25.5 g; 35.8% Cal from Carbo; Fiber 2.2 g; Prot 9.4 g; 13.2% Cal from Prot

Veggie Pizza

2 (8-count) cans refrigerator crescent rolls
16 ounces cream cheese, softened
3/4 cup mayonnaise-type salad dressing
1 envelope ranch salad dressing mix
1 cup chopped broccoli
1 cup chopped tomato
1/2 cup black olives
1/2 cup chopped carrots
2 cups (8 ounces) shredded Cheddar cheese

Unroll the crescent roll dough. Press the dough over the bottom of a baking sheet, pressing the perforations to seal. Bake at 350 degrees for 7 to 8 minutes or until light brown. Let stand until cool.

Combine the cream cheese, salad dressing and salad dressing mix in a bowl and mix until of a spreading consistency. Spread over the baked layer. Sprinkle with the broccoli, tomato, olives and carrots. Top with the cheese and press down lightly. Chill for 1 to 2 hours before serving.

Yield: 10 servings

Nutrients Per Serving: Cal 525; Cal from Fat 365; T Fat 40.6 g; Saturated Fat 19 g; 69.5% Cal from Fat; Chol 79 mg; Sod 1059 mg; T Carbo 27.1 g; 20.6% Cal from Carbo; Fiber 0.7 g; Prot 12.9 g; 9.8% Cal from Prot

Chicken Tikka

2/3 cup natural plain low-fat yogurt
1/4 cup lemon juice
1 tablespoon chopped fresh cilantro
1 teaspoon salt
1 teaspoon ginger paste
1 teaspoon garlic paste
1 teaspoon chili powder
1/4 teaspoon turmeric

31/4 cups chopped boned
   skinned chicken
1 tablespoon vegetable oil
1 small onion, sliced and separated
   into rings for garnish
Lime wedges for garnish
Mixed salad greens for garnish
Sprigs of cilantro for garnish

Combine the yogurt, lemon juice, 1 tablespoon cilantro, the salt, ginger paste, garlic paste, chili powder and turmeric in a bowl and mix well. Add the chicken and stir until coated. Marinate, covered, in the refrigerator for 2 hours, stirring occasionally.

Arrange the chicken on a grill tray or thread the chicken on skewers. Baste with the oil. Grill over medium-hot coals for 15 minutes or until cooked through, turning and basting with the remaining oil two or three times. Garnish with the onion, lime wedges, salad greens and sprigs of cilantro.

Yield: 10 servings

 Nutrients Per Serving: Cal 73; Cal from Fat 19; T Fat 2.3 g; Saturated Fat 0.5 g; 26.2% Cal from Fat; Chol 27 mg; Sod 279 mg; T Carbo 2 g; 11% Cal from Carbo; Fiber 0.1 g; Prot 11.4 g; 62.8% Cal from Prot. *Nutritional profile does not include the ginger paste and garlic paste. Nutritional profile includes all of the marinade.*

FRESH GINGER MAY BE FROZEN FOR UP TO 3 MONTHS, OR IT MAY BE
PEELED, COVERED WITH SHERRY, AND REFRIGERATED.

Barbecups

1 pound ground beef or ground turkey
1/2 cup barbecue sauce
1/4 cup chopped onion
1 to 2 tablespoons brown sugar

1 (10-count) can refrigerator biscuits
1/2 cup (2 ounces) shredded
    Cheddar cheese

Brown the ground beef in a skillet, stirring until crumbly; drain. Stir in the barbecue sauce, onion and brown sugar. Cook until bubbly, stirring occasionally.

Separate the biscuits and pat each biscuit over the bottom and up the side of a muffin cup. Spoon the hot ground beef mixture evenly into the biscuit-lined muffin cups and sprinkle with the cheese. Bake for 10 to 15 minutes or until the crust is golden brown.

Yield: 10 (1-cup) servings

Nutrients Per Serving: Cal 290; Cal from Fat 170; T Fat 18.8 g; Saturated Fat 7.3 g; 58.6% Cal from Fat; Chol 45 mg; Sod 535 mg; T Carbo 18.7 g; 25.8% Cal from Carbo; Fiber 0.3 g; Prot 11.3 g; 15.6% Cal from Prot

Fruit Slush

3 cups water
2 cups sugar
2 cups orange juice (made from
    frozen concentrate)

1 cup crushed pineapple
1 banana, chopped
1 teaspoon lemon juice

Combine the water and sugar in a saucepan and bring to a boil. Boil for 10 minutes. Remove from the heat and let stand until cool. Stir in the orange juice, pineapple, banana and lemon juice. Pour into a freezer container and freeze until of a slushy consistency. Spoon into glasses.

Yield: 12 servings

Nutrients Per Serving: Cal 186; Cal from Fat 2; T Fat 0.2 g; Saturated Fat 0 g; 1.1% Cal from Fat; Chol 0 mg; Sod 0 mg; T Carbo 45.3 g; 97.6% Cal from Carbo; Fiber 0.8 g; Prot 0.6 g; 1.3% Cal from Prot

Red Coat Rally

1 (32-ounce) can pineapple
   juice, chilled
2¼ cups water
¾ cup sugar

1 (6-ounce) can frozen pink lemonade
   concentrate, thawed
1 quart strawberry ice cream
2½ quarts ginger ale

Combine the pineapple juice, water, sugar and lemonade concentrate in a punch bowl and mix well. Add the ice cream and stir until blended. Mix in the ginger ale. Serve immediately in punch cups.

Yield: 12 servings

 Nutrients Per Serving: Cal 231; Cal from Fat 20; T Fat 2.2 g; Saturated Fat 1.3 g; 8.7% Cal from Fat; Chol 9 mg; Sod 31 mg; T Carbo 51.9 g; 89.8% Cal from Carbo; Fiber 0.3 g; Prot 0.9 g; 1.6% Cal from Prot

Dirty Banana

1 ounce rum
1 ounce banana-flavor rum
   or liqueur

¼ cup milk
1 banana, frozen
1½ cups ice

Combine the rum, milk, banana and ice in a blender and process until blended, adding additional rum as needed for the desired strength. Pour evenly into two glasses and serve immediately.

Yield: 2 servings

 Nutrients Per Serving: Cal 71; Cal from Fat 5; T Fat 0.6 g; Saturated Fat 0.4 g; 7% Cal from Fat; Chol 2 mg; Sod 15 mg; T Carbo 15 g; 84.5% Cal from Carbo; Fiber 1.5 g; Prot 1.5 g; 8.5% Cal from Prot

Rum Slush

1 (6-ounce) can frozen orange
   juice concentrate
1 (6-ounce) can frozen
   lemonade concentrate

1/2 cup light rum
3 cups ice, crushed
1 (1-liter) bottle ginger ale

Combine the orange juice concentrate, lemonade concentrate, rum and ice in a blender and process until blended. Spoon the rum mixture into a freezer container and freeze until of a slushy consistency. Spoon the slush mixture evenly into glasses and top off with the ginger ale.

Yield: 12 servings

Nutrients Per Serving: Cal 78; Cal from Fat 0; T Fat 0 g; Saturated Fat 0 g; 0% Cal from Fat; Chol 0 mg; Sod 7 mg; T Carbo 19.2 g; 98.5% Cal from Carbo; Fiber 0.2 g; Prot 0.3 g; 1.5% Cal from Prot

Mulled Christmas Wine

1 (750-milliliter) bottle red wine
2 cinnamon sticks (optional)
2 whole cloves (optional)
1/16 teaspoon ground allspice
1/16 teaspoon nutmeg
1/16 teaspoon ginger

1/16 teaspoon mace
2 cups sugar
Juice of 1 orange
Juice of 1 lemon
1 orange, sliced
1 lemon, sliced

Heat the wine, cinnamon sticks, cloves, allspice, nutmeg, ginger and mace in a large saucepan over medium heat. Stir in the sugar and heat until the sugar dissolves; do not allow to boil. Remove from the heat and let stand for 10 minutes.

Strain the wine mixture through cheesecloth into another saucepan, discarding the solids. Stir in the orange juice and lemon juice. Simmer over low heat for 30 minutes. Mix in the orange slices and lemon slices. Serve warm in mugs.

Yield: 12 servings

Nutrients Per Serving: Cal 156; Cal from Fat 0; T Fat 0 g; Saturated Fat 0 g; 0% Cal from Fat; Chol 0 mg; Sod 2 mg; T Carbo 38.9 g; 99.5% Cal from Carbo; Fiber 0.8 g; Prot 0.2 g; 0.5% Cal from Prot

Lynchburg Lemonade

1/2 (750-milliliter) bottle Jack Daniel's
    Tennessee whiskey
1/2 (750-milliliter) bottle sweet-and-
    sour mix

1/2 (750-milliliter) bottle Triple Sec
1 gallon lemonade
Lemon slices for garnish
Mint leaves for garnish

Combine the liquor, sweet-and-sour mix and liqueur in a large container and mix well. Stir in the lemonade. Pour over ice in glasses and garnish each serving with lemon slices and mint leaves.

Yield: 24 servings

Nutrients Per Serving: Cal 12; Cal from Fat 0; T Fat 0 g; Saturated Fat 0 g; 0% Cal from Fat; Chol 0 mg; Sod 6 mg; T Carbo 3 g; 100% Cal from Carbo; Fiber 0 g; Prot 0 g; 0% Cal from Prot. *Nutritional profile does not include Triple Sec.*

Sangria

2 apples, sliced
2 oranges, sliced
Small ice cubes
1/4 cup superfine sugar
6 ounces Triple Sec

6 ounces brandy
1 (750-milliliter) bottle red wine
1 (750-milliliter) bottle white wine
1 (1-liter) bottle lemon-lime soda

Place the apple slices and orange slices in a large punch bowl and cover with ice cubes. Sprinkle with the sugar and pour the liqueur and brandy over the top. Stir and lightly mash the fruit with the back of a spoon. Add the wine and mix well. Mix in the soda and more ice just before serving. Ladle into glasses.

Yield: 12 servings

Nutrients Per Serving: Cal 93; Cal from Fat 2; T Fat 0.2 g; Saturated Fat 0 g; 2.1% Cal from Fat; Chol 0 mg; Sod 13 mg; T Carbo 22.5 g; 96.6% Cal from Carbo; Fiber 1.4 g; Prot 0.3 g; 1.3% Cal from Prot. *Nutritional profile does not include Triple Sec.*

Breads & Brunch

Colon Cancer

Although not an appetizing subject, any educational material concerning gastrointestinal disorders must address colorectal cancer. At present, it is the second-leading cause of cancer deaths among Americans. According to the American Cancer Society, the incidence of colorectal cancer has decreased 2.1 percent in the last five years. However, it still accounts for 10 percent of all cancer deaths.

Colorectal cancer is a highly preventable disease. The decline in the incidence of colorectal cancer is attributed to the increase in screening and colonoscopies. The American Society for Gastrointestinal Endoscopy estimates that by increasing public awareness of the need for screening and diagnostic colonoscopies, 30,000 lives could be saved annually.

The current recommendations are for all men and women to be screened for colorectal cancer beginning at age fifty. However, if you have a family history of colorectal cancer, a history of polyps, rectal bleeding, or an inflammatory bowel disorder, you need to begin screening sooner. Please discuss this with your physician.

Corn Bread

1 cup yellow cornmeal
1 cup sifted all-purpose flour
1/4 cup sugar
1 tablespoon baking powder
1 teaspoon salt
1/4 cup vegetable shortening
1 cup milk
1 egg, beaten

Combine the cornmeal, flour, sugar, baking powder and salt in a bowl and mix well. Cut the shortening into the cornmeal mixture. Whisk the milk and egg in a bowl until blended and add to the cornmeal mixture. Stir just until moistened.

Spoon the batter into a greased 9×9-inch baking pan. Bake at 425 degrees for 20 to 25 minutes or until light brown. Serve warm.

Yield: 10 servings

Nutrients Per Serving: Cal 180; Cal from Fat 57; T Fat 6.4 g; Saturated Fat 2.6 g; 31.6% Cal from Fat; Chol 26 mg; Sod 400 mg; T Carbo 26.9 g; 59.7% Cal from Carbo; Fiber 1.3 g; Prot 3.9 g; 8.7% Cal from Prot

WHEN STARTING A HIGH-FIBER DIET, IT IS IMPORTANT
TO DO SO GRADUALLY, OR YOU MAY EXPERIENCE INCREASED
GAS, BLOATING, AND CRAMPING.

Scottish Oat Cakes (Cape Breton)

3 cups rolled oats
3 cups all-purpose flour
1 cup sugar
1/2 teaspoon salt
1/2 teaspoon baking powder
1 cup (2 sticks) margarine or butter
1 cup vegetable shortening
1/2 cup hot water

Combine the oats, flour, sugar, salt and baking powder in a bowl and mix well. Cut the margarine into the oat mixture. Mix the shortening and hot water in a bowl and stir into the flour mixture until a dough forms.

Roll the dough 1/8 to 1/4 inch thick on a lightly floured surface. Cut into rounds using a 3-inch cutter. Arrange the rounds in a single layer on a baking sheet and bake at 400 degrees for 10 to 15 minutes or until light brown. Let cool on the baking sheet for 2 minutes and remove to a wire rack.

Yield: 48 (1-cake) servings

 Nutrients Per Serving: Cal 155; Cal from Fat 79; T Fat 8.9 g; Saturated Fat 4.2 g; 50.8% Cal from Fat; Chol 12 mg; Sod 69 mg; T Carbo 16.7 g; 43% Cal from Carbo; Fiber 1.2 g; Prot 2.4 g; 6.2% Cal from Prot

In-and-Out Coffee Cake

Brown Sugar Topping
1/2 cup packed brown sugar
1/2 cup chopped walnuts or pecans (optional)
2 tablespoons butter, melted
1 tablespoon cinnamon

Coffee Cake
2 cups baking mix
3 tablespoons sugar
1 cup milk
1 egg

To prepare the topping, combine the brown sugar, walnuts, butter and cinnamon in a bowl and mix with a fork until crumbly.

To prepare the coffee cake, mix the baking mix and sugar in a bowl. Whisk the milk and egg in a bowl until blended and add to the baking mix mixture. Stir in half the topping.

Spoon the batter into a greased 8×8-inch baking pan and sprinkle evenly with the remaining topping. Bake at 425 degrees for 20 to 25 minutes or until the edges pull from the sides of the pan. Let cool in the pan on a wire rack.

Yield: 8 servings

Nutrients Per Serving: Cal 302; Cal from Fat 120; T Fat 13.1 g; Saturated Fat 3.7 g; 39.7% Cal from Fat; Chol 36 mg; Sod 425 mg; T Carbo 41 g; 54.2% Cal from Carbo; Fiber 1 g; Prot 4.6 g; 6.1% Cal from Prot

Overnight Coffee Cake

Nutty Brown Sugar Topping
1/2 cup packed brown sugar
1/2 cup chopped walnuts
1/2 teaspoon cinnamon
1/4 teaspoon nutmeg

Coffee Cake
2 cups all-purpose flour
2 tablespoons powdered milk

1 teaspoon baking powder
1 teaspoon baking soda
1 teaspoon cinnamon
1/2 teaspoon salt
1 cup granulated sugar
1/2 cup packed brown sugar
2/3 cup margarine
2 eggs, lightly beaten
1 cup buttermilk

To prepare the topping, mix the brown sugar, walnuts, cinnamon and nutmeg in a bowl.

To prepare the coffee cake, mix the flour, powdered milk, baking powder, baking soda, cinnamon and salt in a bowl. Beat the granulated sugar, brown sugar and margarine in a mixing bowl until creamy, scraping the bowl occasionally. Add the eggs and beat until blended. Stir in the buttermilk and flour mixture.

Spoon the batter into a buttered 9x13-inch baking pan and sprinkle with the topping. Chill, covered, for 8 to 10 hours. Bake at 350 degrees for 30 minutes.

Yield: 12 servings

Nutrients Per Serving: Cal 363; Cal from Fat 129; T Fat 14.2 g; Saturated Fat 2.4 g; 35.5% Cal from Fat; Chol 36 mg; Sod 405 mg; T Carbo 53 g; 58.4% Cal from Carbo; Fiber 1.1 g; Prot 5.5 g; 6.1% Cal from Prot

---

LEFTOVER BUTTERMILK MAY BE FROZEN FOR USE IN COOKING, BUT NOT FOR DRINKING. FREEZE BUTTERMILK IN 1/2- TO 1-CUP PORTIONS IN DOUBLE SEALABLE PLASTIC BAGS FOR UP TO 3 MONTHS. THAW IN THE REFRIGERATOR. STIR THE BUTTERMILK IF SEPARATED AFTER THAWING.

Apple Bread

Crumb Topping
1/3 cup all-purpose flour
2 tablespoons granulated sugar
2 tablespoons brown sugar
1/2 teaspoon cinnamon
1/4 cup (1/2 stick) butter

Bread
2 1/2 cups all-purpose flour
2 teaspoons cinnamon
1 teaspoon baking soda

1 teaspoon baking powder
1 teaspoon salt
1 1/2 cups packed brown sugar
2/3 cup vegetable oil
1 egg
1 cup buttermilk
1 1/2 cups finely chopped Winesap
   apples, Nittany apples, or
   Rome apples
1 cup chopped walnuts or pecans
1 teaspoon vanilla extract

To prepare the topping, combine the flour, granulated sugar, brown sugar and cinnamon in a bowl. Cut the butter into the flour mixture until crumbly.

To prepare the bread, mix the flour, cinnamon, baking soda, baking powder and salt in a bowl. Combine the brown sugar, oil and egg in a mixing bowl and beat until creamy, scraping the bowl occasionally. Add the flour mixture and buttermilk alternately to the creamed mixture, mixing well after each addition. Stir in the apples, walnuts and vanilla.

Spoon the batter evenly into two greased 5x9-inch loaf pans and sprinkle with the topping. Bake at 325 degrees for 60 minutes. Let cool in the pans for 10 minutes. Remove to a wire rack to cool completely.

Yield: 20 (1-slice) servings

Nutrients Per Serving: Cal 277; Cal from Fat 121; T Fat 13.7 g; Saturated Fat 2.7 g; 43.7% Cal from Fat; Chol 17 mg; Sod 251 mg; T Carbo 35 g; 50.5% Cal from Carbo; Fiber 1.1 g; Prot 4 g; 5.8% Cal from Prot

Apricot Cranberry Bread

2 cups all-purpose flour
1 cup sugar
1 to 2 teaspoons grated orange zest
1 1/2 teaspoons baking powder
1/2 teaspoon baking soda
1/2 teaspoon salt
3/4 cup water
1/4 cup vegetable oil
1 egg
1 cup fresh or frozen cranberry halves
1/4 cup apricot preserves

Combine the flour, sugar, orange zest, baking powder, baking soda and salt in a bowl and mix well. Whisk the water, oil and egg in a large bowl until blended. Stir in the flour mixture and fold in the cranberries.

Spoon the batter into a greased and floured 5×9-inch loaf pan. Cut the apricots in the preserves into smaller pieces. Spoon the preserves over the batter and cut through the batter with a knife to swirl. Bake at 350 degrees for 65 to 70 minutes or until a wooden pick inserted near the center comes out clean. Let cool in the pan for 10 minutes. Remove to a wire rack to cool completely.

Yield: 12 (1-slice) servings

 Nutrients Per Serving: Cal 211; Cal from Fat 47; T Fat 5.1 g; Saturated Fat 0.7 g; 22.2% Cal from Fat; Chol 18 mg; Sod 219 mg; T Carbo 38.4 g; 72.7% Cal from Carbo; Fiber 1.1 g; Prot 2.7 g; 5.1% Cal from Prot

Boston Brown Bread

1/2 cup golden raisins
1/2 cup apple cider
1/2 cup yellow cornmeal
1/2 cup whole wheat flour
6 tablespoons rye flour
2 tablespoons wheat bran
1 teaspoon baking soda

1/2 teaspoon salt
1 cup buttermilk
1/3 cup dark molasses
2 tablespoons honey
2 tablespoons apple cider
1/2 cup grated carrots

Plump the raisins in 1/2 cup cider in a bowl for 15 minutes; drain. Mix the cornmeal, whole wheat flour, rye flour, wheat bran, baking soda and salt in a large bowl. Mix the buttermilk, molasses, honey and 2 tablespoons apple cider in a bowl and mix until blended. Add to the cornmeal mixture and mix well. Stir in the raisins and carrots.

Spoon the batter into a generously buttered coffee can and cover with double thickness foil. Place the can foil side up in a saucepan and add enough boiling water to the saucepan to reach halfway up the side of the can. Cover the can with a saucepan of comparable size and steam over medium-low heat for 1 1/2 hours or until a wooden pick inserted in the center of the bread comes out clean. Let cool on a wire rack for at least 10 minutes before removing the bread from the can.

Yield: 10 (1-slice) servings

Nutrients Per Serving: Cal 155; Cal from Fat 5; T Fat 0.5 g; Saturated Fat 0.1 g; 3.2% Cal from Fat; Chol 1 mg; Sod 277 mg; T Carbo 34.5 g; 88.8% Cal from Carbo; Fiber 2.6 g; Prot 3.1 g; 8% Cal from Prot

Carrot Cake Bread

2¹/₂ cups all-purpose flour
1 cup quick-cooking oats
1 cup packed brown sugar
1 tablespoon baking powder
¹/₂ teaspoon cinnamon
¹/₄ teaspoon salt
1¹/₂ cups grated carrots
¹/₂ cup raisins
¹/₂ cup milk
1 teaspoon vanilla extract

Combine the flour, oats, brown sugar, baking powder, cinnamon and salt in a bowl and mix well. Add the carrots, raisins, milk and vanilla to the flour mixture and stir just until moistened.

Spoon the batter into a 5x9-inch loaf pan and bake at 350 degrees for 55 to 60 minutes or until the loaf tests done. Let cool in the pan for 15 to 20 minutes and remove to a wire rack to cool completely.

Yield: 10 (1-slice) servings

Nutrients Per Serving: Cal 272; Cal from Fat 10; T Fat 1 g; Saturated Fat 0.2 g; 3.7% Cal from Fat; Chol 1 mg; Sod 229 mg; T Carbo 60.2 g; 88.4% Cal from Carbo; Fiber 2.7 g; Prot 5.4 g; 7.9% Cal from Prot

Zucchini Bread

3 cups all-purpose flour
2 teaspoons baking soda
1 1/2 teaspoons cinnamon
1 teaspoon salt
1/2 teaspoon baking powder
3/4 cup nuts (optional)
3 eggs
2 cups sugar
1 cup vegetable oil
2 teaspoons vanilla extract
2 cups loosely packed grated peeled zucchini
1 (8-ounce) can crushed pineapple, drained

Mix the flour, baking soda, cinnamon, salt and baking powder in a bowl. Add the nuts and toss to coat. Beat the eggs in a mixing bowl until blended. Add the sugar, oil and vanilla and beat until creamy. Add the flour mixture and beat just until moistened. Stir in the zucchini and pineapple.

Spoon the batter into two greased 5×9-inch loaf pans. Bake at 350 degrees for 55 to 60 minutes or until the loaves test done. Let cool in the pans for 10 minutes. Remove to a wire rack to cool completely.

Yield: 20 (1-slice) servings

Nutrients Per Serving: Cal 265; Cal from Fat 107; T Fat 11.8 g; Saturated Fat 1.6 g; 40.4% Cal from Fat; Chol 32 mg; Sod 265 mg; T Carbo 36.5 g; 55.2% Cal from Carbo; Fiber 0.8 g; Prot 2.9 g; 4.4% Cal from Prot

Pumpkin Muffins

1¹/₂ cups all-purpose flour
1 teaspoon baking powder
¹/₂ teaspoon baking soda
¹/₂ teaspoon salt
¹/₄ teaspoon ground cloves
¹/₄ teaspoon cinnamon

1 cup sugar
³/₄ cup pumpkin
¹/₄ cup vegetable oil
2 eggs
³/₄ cup raisins
¹/₂ cup chopped walnuts

Sift the flour, baking powder, baking soda, salt, cloves and cinnamon into a bowl and mix well. Combine the sugar, pumpkin, oil and eggs in a bowl and mix well. Add the flour mixture and stir just until moistened. Fold in the raisins and walnuts. Fill greased muffin cups two-thirds full. Bake at 400 degrees for 18 to 20 minutes or until golden brown.

Yield: 12 (1-muffin) servings

Nutrients Per Serving: Cal 248; Cal from Fat 77; T Fat 8.6 g; Saturated Fat 1.2 g; 31% Cal from Fat; Chol 35 mg; Sod 203 mg; T Carbo 39 g; 62.9% Cal from Carbo; Fiber 1.4 g; Prot 3.8 g; 6.1% Cal from Prot

THE VIVID ORANGE COLOR OF PUMPKIN INDICATES A HIGH CONTENT OF
CAROTENE PIGMENTS, SUCH AS LUTEIN, ALPHA-CAROTENE, AND BETA-CAROTENE
(WHICH TURNS INTO VITAMIN A IN THE BODY).

English Muffin Bread

5^1/$_2$ to 6 cups all-purpose flour
2 envelopes dry yeast
1 tablespoon sugar
2 teaspoons salt
^{1}/$_2$ teaspoon baking soda
2 cups milk (120 to 130 degrees)
^{1}/$_2$ cup water (120 to 130 degrees)
^{1}/$_2$ cup cornmeal

Combine 3 cups of the flour, the yeast, sugar, salt and baking soda in a large mixing bowl. Add the heated milk and heated water to the flour mixture and beat until blended. Add enough of the remaining flour to make a stiff but moist dough and mix well.

Grease two 5×9-inch loaf pans and sprinkle enough of the cornmeal over the sides of the pans to coat. Spoon the batter evenly into the prepared loaf pans and sprinkle the remaining cornmeal over the top. Let rise, covered with damp tea towels, for 45 minutes. Bake at 400 degrees for 25 minutes. Remove the loaves to a wire rack to cool. Slice and toast and serve with butter and jam.

Yield: 20 (1-slice) servings

Nutrients Per Serving: Cal 162; Cal from Fat 8; T Fat 1 g; Saturated Fat 0.4 g; 4.9% Cal from Fat; Chol 2 mg; Sod 280 mg; T Carbo 33.3 g; 82.2% Cal from Carbo; Fiber 1.4 g; Prot 5.2 g; 12.8% Cal from Prot. *Nutritional profile includes all of the flour.*

Sally Lunn Bread

1 envelope dry yeast
1/2 cup warm water (105 to 115 degrees)
51/2 to 6 cups all-purpose flour
1 cup milk, heated
1/2 cup (1 stick) butter or margarine, softened
1/4 cup sugar
3 eggs at room temperature, beaten
2 teaspoons salt

Dissolve the yeast in the water in a large mixing bowl. Add 2 cups of the flour, the milk, butter, sugar, eggs and salt and beat until blended. Add the remaining flour gradually until the dough is elastic and easy to handle.

Let rise, covered with a damp tea towel, for 1 hour or until doubled in bulk. Punch down the dough and spoon evenly into a greased 10-inch tube pan or two greased 5×9-inch loaf pans. Let rise, covered, with a damp tea towel, for 1 hour or until doubled in bulk.

Bake the tube pan at 400 degrees for 30 minutes or bake the loaf pans at 375 degrees for 30 minutes. Let cool in the pan or pans for 10 minutes and remove to a wire rack to cool completely.

Yield: 16 servings

Nutrients Per Serving: Cal 253; Cal from Fat 67; T Fat 7.5 g; Saturated Fat 4.2 g; 26.5% Cal from Fat; Chol 57 mg; Sod 375 mg; T Carbo 39.8 g; 62.9% Cal from Carbo; Fiber 1.4 g; Prot 6.7 g; 10.6% Cal from Prot. *Nutritional profile includes all of the flour.*

Bacon, Egg and Cheese Squares

12 slices Canadian bacon or baked ham
12 slices Swiss cheese or American cheese
12 eggs
1 cup light cream
1/2 cup (2 ounces) grated Parmesan cheese

Line the bottom of a 9×13-inch baking pan with the bacon and top with the Swiss cheese. Crack the eggs over the prepared layers in a single layer, being careful not to break the yolks. Drizzle the cream over the whites just until the yolks peek through.

Bake at 425 degrees for 20 minutes. Sprinkle with the Parmesan cheese and bake for 8 to 10 minutes longer. Cut into squares and serve immediately.

Yield: 12 servings

Nutrients Per Serving: Cal 230; Cal from Fat 150; T Fat 16.7 g; Saturated Fat 8.5 g; 65.1% Cal from Fat; Chol 253 mg; Sod 463 mg; T Carbo 2.4 g; 4.2% Cal from Carbo; Fiber 0 g; Prot 17.7 g; 30.7% Cal from Prot

Overnight Sausage Casserole

2 pounds bulk pork sausage
2 cups milk
8 eggs, beaten
1 teaspoon dry mustard
2 cups (8 ounces) shredded sharp Cheddar cheese
8 slices white bread

Brown the sausage in a skillet, stirring until crumbly; drain. Whisk the milk, eggs and dry mustard in a bowl until blended and pour into a greased 9×13-inch baking pan. Sprinkle the sausage and cheese over the egg mixture.

Tear the bread slices into pieces about the size of a quarter and arrange on top of the prepared layers. Chill, covered, for 8 to 10 hours. Remove the cover and bake at 350 degrees for 45 to 60 minutes.

Yield: 12 servings

Nutrients Per Serving: Cal 508; Cal from Fat 374; T Fat 41.7 g; Saturated Fat 16.6 g; 73.6% Cal from Fat; Chol 215 mg; Sod 785 mg; T Carbo 12.9 g; 10.2% Cal from Carbo; Fiber 0.4 g; Prot 20.6 g; 16.2% Cal from Prot

SUBSTITUTING WHOLE GRAIN BREAD FOR WHITE BREAD
AND WHOLE WHEAT PASTA FOR REGULAR ARE GREAT WAYS TO INCREASE
FIBER CONSUMPTION.

Sausage and Egg Scramble

1 pound bulk pork sausage
10 ounces (2 cups) seasoned diced
    home fries
1/3 cup chopped green bell pepper

1/3 cup chopped red bell pepper
8 eggs
1/2 cup milk

Brown the sausage with the potatoes and bell peppers in a large skillet over medium heat, stirring until the sausage is crumbly and the potatoes are brown; drain. Whisk the eggs and milk in a bowl until blended.

Pour the egg mixture over the sausage mixture. Cook until the eggs are cooked through, gently stirring. Serve warm.

Yield: 6 servings

Nutrients Per Serving: Cal 484; Cal from Fat 342; T Fat 37.9 g; Saturated Fat 13.2 g; 70.7% Cal from Fat; Chol 334 mg; Sod 612 mg; T Carbo 16 g; 13.2% Cal from Carbo; Fiber 1.3 g; Prot 19.4 g; 16% Cal from Prot

Sausage Potato Bake

1 1/4 cups milk
5 eggs, beaten
1/4 teaspoon salt
8 ounces sausage links, sliced

3 1/2 cups frozen O'Brien potatoes
1 1/2 cups (6 ounces) shredded
    Cheddar cheese

Whisk the milk, eggs and salt in a bowl until blended. Stir in the sausage, potatoes and cheese. Spoon into a greased 9×13-inch baking dish.

Bake at 350 degrees for 50 minutes or until a knife inserted in the center comes out clean. Let stand for 10 minutes before serving.

Yield: 12 servings

Nutrients Per Serving: Cal 230; Cal from Fat 135; T Fat 15 g; Saturated Fat 6.6 g; 58.6% Cal from Fat; Chol 118 mg; Sod 324 mg; T Carbo 13.5 g; 23.5% Cal from Carbo; Fiber 1.3 g; Prot 10.3 g; 17.9% Cal from Prot

Ham and Cheese Quiche

1/2 cup chopped onion
1 tablespoon butter
1 cup milk
6 eggs, lightly beaten
8 ounces cooked ham, chopped
8 ounces Swiss cheese, chopped
3/4 cup sour cream
1 teaspoon salt
1/8 teaspoon nutmeg
1/8 teaspoon pepper
2 unbaked (9-inch) pie shells

Sauté the onion in the butter in a skillet. Whisk the milk and eggs in a bowl until blended and stir in the sautéed onion, ham, cheese, sour cream, salt, nutmeg and pepper. Spoon evenly into the pie shells.

Bake at 450 degrees for 10 minutes. Reduce the heat to 325 degrees and bake for 20 to 25 minutes longer or until set. Cut into wedges to serve.

Yield: 16 servings

Nutrients Per Serving: Cal 271; Cal from Fat 163; T Fat 18.2 g; Saturated Fat 8.9 g; 60.2% Cal from Fat; Chol 107 mg; Sod 422 mg; T Carbo 15.3 g; 22.6% Cal from Carbo; Fiber 0.1 g; Prot 11.6 g; 17.1% Cal from Prot

Asparagus Quiche

2/3 *pound thin asparagus spears*
2 *teaspoons olive oil*
1/4 *cup minced shallots*
8 *ounces Gruyère cheese or Swiss cheese, shredded*
1 *cup milk*
5 *eggs*
2 *tablespoons dry white wine (optional)*
1/2 *teaspoon salt*
1/2 *teaspoon thyme*
1/4 *teaspoon pepper*

Snap off the woody ends of the asparagus spears and discard. Cut the spears into 1/2-inch pieces. Heat the olive oil in a skillet and add the shallots. Sauté until tender. Layer the cheese evenly in a 14-inch pie plate sprayed with nonstick cooking spray. Top with the asparagus.

Whisk the milk, eggs, wine, salt, thyme and pepper in a bowl until blended. Stir in the shallots and pour over the prepared layers. Bake at 350 degrees for 45 minutes or until slightly puffed and light brown.

Note: You may bake the quiche in a pie shell. Reduce the fat grams by substituting with reduced-fat cheese.

Yield: 8 servings

 Nutrients Per Serving: Cal 190; Cal from Fat 114; T Fat 12.7 g; Saturated Fat 6.6 g; 59.9% Cal from Fat; Chol 160 mg; Sod 276 mg; T Carbo 5.1 g; 10.7% Cal from Carbo; Fiber 0.9 g; Prot 14 g; 29.4% Cal from Prot

Spinach and Gruyère Casserole

1 (10-ounce) package frozen chopped
    spinach, thawed and drained
8 to 10 (1/2-inch) slices French or
    Italian bread
2 tablespoons unsalted butter, softened
4 shallots, minced (about 1/2 cup)
2 tablespoons unsalted butter, softened
Salt and freshly ground pepper to taste
1/2 cup medium-dry white wine, such
    as sauvignon blanc

1 tablespoon unsalted butter, softened
1 cup (4 ounces) shredded Gruyère
    cheese or other Swiss cheese
13/4 cups half-and-half
6 eggs
1 teaspoon salt
1/2 cup (2 ounces) shredded Gruyère
    cheese or other Swiss cheese

Press any excess moisture from the spinach. Arrange the bread slices in a single layer on a large baking sheet. Place the baking sheet on the middle oven rack and toast at 225 degrees for 40 minutes or until the bread is dry and crisp, turning the slices after 20 minutes. Let stand until cool and brush one side of each of the slices with 2 tablespoons butter.

Sauté the shallots in 2 tablespoons butter in a nonstick skillet over medium heat for 3 minutes or until tender.

Stir in the spinach and salt and pepper to taste. Cook for 2 minutes or until combined. Remove the spinach mixture to a bowl. Add the wine to the skillet and increase the heat to medium-high. Simmer for 3 minutes or until the wine is reduced to 1/4 cup.

Coat an 8x8-inch baking dish with 1 tablespoon butter. Layer the bread slices in a single layer butter side up, the spinach and 1 cup cheese half at a time in the prepared baking dish. Whisk the reduced wine, half-and-half, eggs, 1 teaspoon salt and pepper in a bowl until blended. Pour the egg mixture over the prepared layers and cover with plastic wrap. Weight the layers down with two 1-pound packages of confectioners' sugar or a plastic bag filled with two pounds of rice or sugar. Chill for 1 to 10 hours.

Let stand at room temperature for 20 minutes and sprinkle with 1/2 cup cheese. Bake at 325 degrees for 50 to 55 minutes or until the edges and center are puffed and the edges have pulled slightly from the sides of the baking dish. Let cool on a wire rack for 5 minutes before serving. You may substitute minced yellow onion for the minced shallots.

Yield: 6 servings

Nutrients Per Serving: Cal 481; Cal from Fat 305; T Fat 33.8 g; Saturated Fat 18.8 g; 63.4% Cal from Fat; Chol 296 mg; Sod 800 mg; T Carbo 22.4 g; 18.6% Cal from Carbo; Fiber 2.4 g; Prot 21.6 g; 18% Cal from Prot

Soups & Salads

Constipation

Constipation is a condition in which a person's bowels move less than three times per week and the stool is frequently dry and hard. Constipation usually results from excess water being absorbed as the stool passes slowly through the colon or large intestine. Any alteration or deviation from one's normal routine may result in an episode of constipation. Such changes may be dietary in nature, an altered exercise routine, a sedentary lifestyle, or even an increasing stress level. Other possible causes of constipation could include certain medications such as narcotics, iron supplements, and common medications for blood pressure and heart disease.

Beef Chili with Kidney Beans

2 tablespoons vegetable oil or corn oil
2 cups chopped onions
1 red bell pepper, cut into
   1/2-inch pieces
6 garlic cloves, minced
   (about 2 tablespoons)
1/4 cup chili powder
1 tablespoon ground cumin
2 teaspoons coriander
1 teaspoon dried oregano

1 teaspoon red pepper flakes
1/2 teaspoon cayenne pepper
2 pounds lean ground beef
2 (16-ounce) cans dark red kidney
   beans, drained and rinsed
1 (28-ounce) can diced tomatoes
1 (28-ounce) can tomato purée
1/2 teaspoon salt
Salt to taste

Heat the oil in a large Dutch oven over medium heat for 3 to 4 minutes or until simmering but not smoking. Stir in the onions, bell pepper, garlic, chili powder, cumin, coriander, oregano, red pepper flakes and cayenne pepper and mix well.

Cook for 10 minutes or until the vegetables are tender and just beginning to brown. Increase the heat to medium-high and add half the ground beef. Cook for 3 to 4 minutes or until the ground beef is just beginning to brown, stirring constantly with a wooden spoon. Add the remaining ground beef and cook, stirring constantly, for 3 to 4 minutes longer or until the ground beef is crumbly. Stir in the beans, undrained tomatoes, tomato purée and 1/2 teaspoon salt. Bring to a boil and reduce the heat to low.

Simmer, covered, for 1 hour, stirring occasionally. Remove the cover and simmer for 1 hour longer or until the chili is slightly thickened, stirring occasionally. If the beans stick to the bottom of the pan, stir in 1/2 cup water and continue to simmer. Taste and season with salt to taste. Serve with lime wedges and additional toppings such as chopped fresh tomatoes, chopped avocados, chopped red onions, chopped fresh cilantro, shredded Monterey Jack cheese or Cheddar cheese and/or sour cream.

Yield: 10 servings

Nutrients Per Serving: Cal 1381; Cal from Fat 267; T Fat 29.7 g; Saturated Fat 8.9 g; 19.3% Cal from Fat; Chol 67 mg; Sod 3911 mg; T Carbo 213.5 g; 61.9% Cal from Carbo; Fiber 55.4 g; Prot 64.9 g; 18.8% Cal from Prot

Taco Soup

1 pound ground beef
1 to 2 teaspoons chili powder
1 teaspoon ground cumin
3 cups beef broth
1 (16-ounce) jar picante sauce
1 (14-ounce) can diced tomatoes
1 onion, chopped
1 cup rotini
1 small green bell pepper, chopped
2 garlic cloves, minced
2 cups (8 ounces) shredded Cheddar cheese

Brown the ground beef in a Dutch oven, stirring until crumbly; drain. Sprinkle the chili powder and cumin over the ground beef and cook for 30 seconds, stirring constantly. Stir in the broth, picante sauce, undrained tomatoes, onion, pasta, bell pepper and garlic and bring to a boil, stirring frequently. Reduce the heat to low.

Simmer, covered, for 15 minutes or until the pasta is tender, stirring occasionally. Ladle into bowls and sprinkle evenly with the cheese. Serve with tortilla chips.

Yield: 8 servings

Nutrients Per Serving: Cal 714; Cal from Fat 356; T Fat 39.6 g; Saturated Fat 14.8 g; 49.9% Cal from Fat; Chol 77 mg; Sod 1563 mg; T Carbo 61.9 g; 34.7% Cal from Carbo; Fiber 7.1 g; Prot 27.5 g; 15.4% Cal from Prot

Spicy Beefy Cheese Soup

1 pound ground beef
16 ounces processed cheese, cubed
1 (15-ounce) can kidney beans
1 (14-ounce) can stewed tomatoes
1 (8-ounce) can whole kernel corn
1 jalapeño chile, seeded and chopped (optional)
1 envelope taco seasoning mix

Brown the ground beef in a skillet, stirring until crumbly; drain. Combine the ground beef, cheese, undrained beans, undrained tomatoes, undrained corn, jalapeño chile and taco seasoning mix in a slow cooker and mix well. Cook, covered, on Low for 4 to 5 hours or on High for 3 hours. Ladle into soup bowls and serve with corn chips.

Yield: 8 servings

Nutrients Per Serving: Cal 433; Cal from Fat 248; T Fat 27.7 g; Saturated Fat 13.7 g; 57.2% Cal from Fat; Chol 79 mg; Sod 1493 mg; T Carbo 23.6 g; 21.8% Cal from Carbo; Fiber 3 g; Prot 22.7 g; 21% Cal from Prot

Kielbasa Lentil Soup

1 cup dried navy beans, sorted
  and rinsed
1 pound lentils, sorted
8 cups water
2 (16-ounce) cans diced tomatoes
2 bay leaves
1 tablespoon salt

1/4 teaspoon pepper
1 1/2 pounds kielbasa,
  sliced or chopped
8 slices bacon, chopped
1/2 cup chopped carrots
1/2 cup chopped celery
1 onion, sliced

Combine the beans, lentils and water in a stockpot and bring to a boil. Reduce the heat and cook until the beans and lentils are almost tender. Stir in the tomatoes, bay leaves, salt and pepper. Reduce the heat to low and stir in the sausage. Simmer for 15 minutes, stirring occasionally.

Fry the bacon in a skillet until crisp-cooked. Drain, reserving 1 tablespoon of the bacon drippings. Crumble the bacon. Cook the bacon, carrots, celery and onion in the reserved bacon drippings for 15 minutes, stirring frequently. Mix the bacon mixture into the bean mixture and cook for 30 minutes, stirring occasionally. Discard the bay leaves and ladle the soup into soup bowls.

Yield: 8 servings

Nutrients Per Serving: Cal 638; Cal from Fat 250; T Fat 27.7 g; Saturated Fat 9.7 g; 39.2% Cal from Fat; Chol 65 mg; Sod 2111 mg; T Carbo 61.6 g; 38.6% Cal from Carbo; Fiber 15 g; Prot 35.4 g; 22.2% Cal from Prot

---

TO INCREASE FIBER INTAKE, TRY RECIPES THAT CONTAIN 5 GRAMS
OR MORE OF FIBER PER SERVING.

Chicken Corn Soup

1 (3-pound) chicken, or 2 whole chicken breasts
12 cups water
1 cup chopped onion
1 rib celery, chopped
1 tablespoon salt
1/4 teaspoon pepper
1 (16-ounce) package frozen corn or
    fresh whole kernel corn
1 cup all-purpose flour
1/16 teaspoon salt
1 egg, lightly beaten
1/16 teaspoon parsley

Bring the chicken, water, onion, celery, 1 tablespoon salt and the pepper to a boil in a stockpot and reduce the heat to low. Simmer for 2 hours or until the chicken is cooked through. Remove the chicken to a platter and let cool slightly. Chop the chicken into bite-size pieces or shred, discarding the skin and bones. Skim the fat from the broth and stir in the corn. Cook until the corn is tender.

Mix the flour and 1/16 teaspoon salt in a bowl. Add the egg and stir until blended. Shape the dough into rounds the size of a marble. Drop the rounds into the boiling soup and boil for 15 minutes. Stir in the chicken and parsley and ladle into soup bowls.

Yield: 12 servings

Nutrients Per Serving: Cal 278; Cal from Fat 102; T Fat 11.3 g; Saturated Fat 3.1 g; 36.7% Cal from Fat; Chol 91 mg; Sod 698 mg; T Carbo 17.4 g; 25% Cal from Carbo; Fiber 1.5 g; Prot 26.6 g; 38.3% Cal from Prot

Manhattan Clam Chowder

4 slices bacon, chopped
1 cup sliced onion
1 cup chopped carrots
1 cup chopped celery
1 tablespoon chopped parsley
1 (12-ounce) can tomatoes
1 (11-ounce) jar clams
2 teaspoons salt
4 peppercorns
1 bay leaf
1 1/4 teaspoons dried thyme leaves
3 potatoes, peeled and chopped

Sauté the bacon in a large Dutch oven until almost crisp. Add the onion and cook for 5 minutes or until the onion is tender. Stir in the carrots, celery and parsley. Cook over low heat for 5 minutes, stirring occasionally.

Drain the tomatoes, reserving the juice. Pour the reserved juice into a 2-quart measuring cup. Add the tomatoes to the carrot mixture. Drain the clams, reserving the liquid. Add the reserved liquid to the reserved tomato juice. Add enough water to the juice mixture to measure 1 1/2 quarts and add to the chowder. Stir in the salt, peppercorns, bay leaf and thyme. Bring to a boil and reduce the heat to low.

Simmer for 45 minutes and stir in the potatoes. Simmer, covered, for 20 minutes. Chop the clams and add to the chowder. Simmer for 15 minutes longer, stirring occasionally. Discard the peppercorns and bay leaf and ladle the chowder into soup bowls.

Yield: 8 servings

Nutrients Per Serving: Cal 138; Cal from Fat 20; T Fat 2.4 g; Saturated Fat 0.8 g; 14.5% Cal from Fat; Chol 32 mg; Sod 984 mg; T Carbo 20.1 g; 58.1% Cal from Carbo; Fiber 2.8 g; Prot 9.5 g; 27.5% Cal from Prot

Cream of Crab Soup

1 small onion, chopped
1 tablespoon butter or margarine
1 cup strong chicken stock
4 cups milk
1 tablespoon finely chopped parsley
1 teaspoon celery salt
1/2 teaspoon mace
1/8 teaspoon red pepper
Salt and black pepper to taste
1 pound crab meat, drained and flaked
2 tablespoons all-purpose flour
1/4 cup sherry (optional)

Sauté the onion in the butter in a stockpot until the onion is tender. Stir in the stock. Add the milk gradually, stirring constantly. Stir in the parsley, celery salt, mace, red pepper, salt and black pepper. Add the crab meat and simmer for 15 minutes.

Whisk the flour with just enough water in a bowl to make a thin paste. Stir the flour mixture into the soup and cook until slightly thickened, stirring frequently. Stir in the sherry just before serving. Ladle into soup bowls.

Yield: 6 servings

Nutrients Per Serving: Cal 187; Cal from Fat 56; T Fat 6.2 g; Saturated Fat 3.4 g; 29.9% Cal from Fat; Chol 76 mg; Sod 589 mg; T Carbo 11.4 g; 24.4% Cal from Carbo; Fiber 0.3 g; Prot 21.4 g; 45.7% Cal from Prot

She-Crab Soup

1 quart (4 cups) whipping cream
1/8 teaspoon salt
1/8 teaspoon pepper
2 fish bouillon cubes
2 cups boiling water
1/4 cup (1/2 stick) unsalted butter
1/3 cup all-purpose flour
2 tablespoons lemon juice
1/4 teaspoon Old Bay seasoning
1 pound fresh crab meat, drained and flaked
1/3 cup sherry for garnish
Chopped parsley for garnish

Bring the cream, salt and pepper to a boil in a heavy saucepan over medium heat. Reduce the heat to low and simmer for 1 hour. Dissolve the bouillon cubes in the water in a heatproof bowl.

Melt the butter in a saucepan over low heat and stir in the flour. Cook for 1 minute or until smooth and bubbly, stirring constantly. Add the hot fish bouillon gradually and cook over medium heat until thickened, stirring frequently. Stir in the cream mixture and cook until heated through. Add the lemon juice, Old Bay seasoning and crab meat and mix well. Cook just until heated through. Ladle into soup bowls and garnish evenly with the sherry and parsley.

Yield: 6 servings

 Nutrients Per Serving: Cal 438; Cal from Fat 342; T Fat 38.1 g; Saturated Fat 23.3 g; 78.1% Cal from Fat; Chol 189 mg; Sod 341 mg; T Carbo 7.9 g; 7.2% Cal from Carbo; Fiber 0.2 g; Prot 16.1 g; 14.7% Cal from Prot

Vegetable Crab Soup

1 onion, grated
2 tablespoons butter
1 tablespoon all-purpose flour
3 cups chicken bouillon
1 teaspoon Worcestershire sauce
1 to 5 drops of Tabasco sauce
$1/16$ teaspoon Old Bay seasoning
Salt and pepper to taste
Paprika to taste
1 pound crab meat, drained and flaked
1 potato, chopped
1 carrot, chopped
2 ribs celery, chopped
2 cups tomato juice

Brown the onion in the butter in a saucepan and stir in the flour. Cook until bubbly and of a paste consistency, stirring constantly. Add the bouillon, Worcestershire sauce, Tabasco sauce, Old Bay seasoning, salt, pepper and paprika and mix well. Stir in the crab meat, potato, carrot, and celery.

Simmer for 15 minutes, stirring occasionally. Stir in the tomato juice and simmer for 5 minutes longer or until the vegetables are tender. Ladle into soup bowls.

Yield: 6 servings

Nutrients Per Serving: Cal 167; Cal from Fat 43; T Fat 4.7 g; Saturated Fat 2.6 g; 25.8% Cal from Fat; Chol 69 mg; Sod 996 mg; T Carbo 14.9 g; 35.8% Cal from Carbo; Fiber 2 g; Prot 16 g; 38.4% Cal from Prot

Oyster Stew

1 pint fresh oysters
1/2 teaspoon minced onion
1/4 cup (1/2 stick) butter or margarine
1 tablespoon all-purpose flour
4 cups fat-free milk
1 (10-ounce) can cream of mushroom soup
1/8 teaspoon Worcestershire sauce
Salt and pepper to taste

Drain the oysters, reserving the liquor. Sauté the oysters and onion in the butter in a saucepan until the edges of the oysters begin to curl. Stir in the flour until combined. Add the reserved liquor, the milk, soup and Worcestershire sauce and mix well.

Cook until heated through, stirring occasionally; do not boil. Season with salt and pepper and ladle into soup bowls.

Yield: 4 servings

 Nutrients Per Serving: Cal 312; Cal from Fat 170; T Fat 18.9 g; Saturated Fat 9 g; 54.5% Cal from Fat; Chol 64 mg; Sod 797 mg; T Carbo 18.6 g; 23.8% Cal from Carbo; Fiber 0.3 g; Prot 16.9 g; 21.7% Cal from Prot

AS THE SECOND-LEADING CAUSE OF CANCER DEATHS AMONG AMERICANS,
COLORECTAL CANCER IS ONE OF THE MOST PREVENTABLE CANCERS AS WELL AS ONE
OF THE MOST CURABLE CANCERS WHEN DETECTED AT AN EARLY STAGE.

Creamy Shrimp and Artichoke Soup

2 (10-ounce) cans cream of shrimp soup
3 cups milk
8 ounces Velveeta cheese or
   Velveeta Mexican cheese, cubed
1 (14-ounce) can artichoke hearts,
   drained and chopped
1/2 teaspoon Beau Monde seasoning
1/4 teaspoon seasoned salt
1/4 teaspoon white pepper
2 (5-ounce) packages frozen cooked
   small shrimp
Sherry to taste (optional)
Red bell pepper strips for garnish
Chopped fresh parsley for garnish

Combine the soup, milk, cheese, artichokes, Beau Monde seasoning, salt and white pepper in a Dutch oven and mix gently. Cook over low heat until the cheese melts and the soup is hot, stirring frequently. Stir in the shrimp and cook for 1 minute longer or until heated through. Stir in sherry and ladle into soup bowls. Garnish with bell pepper strips and parsley.

Note: May be prepared up to 1 day in advance, excluding the addition of the shrimp and sherry, and stored, covered, in the refrigerator. Reheat the soup and add the shrimp and sherry just before serving.

Yield: 8 servings

Nutrients Per Serving: Cal 228; Cal from Fat 102; T Fat 11.4 g; Saturated Fat 6.7 g; 44.7% Cal from Fat; Chol 53 mg; Sod 1315 mg; T Carbo 15 g; 26.3% Cal from Carbo; Fiber 0.9 g; Prot 16.6 g; 29.1% Cal from Prot. *Nutritional profile does not include Beau Monde seasoning.*

Raspberry Yogurt Soup

2 (10-ounce) packages frozen sweetened raspberries or
    strawberries, partially thawed
2 cups plain nonfat yogurt
1/4 teaspoon cinnamon

Process the raspberries in a food processor or blender until puréed. Strain to remove the seeds, if desired. Add the yogurt and cinnamon and process just until combined. Serve cold in chilled soup bowls.

Note: This soup is great for brunch or for luncheons.

Yield: 4 servings

Nutrients Per Serving: Cal 222; Cal from Fat 4; T Fat 0.4 g; Saturated Fat 0.1 g; 1.8% Cal from Fat; Chol 2 mg; Sod 95 mg; T Carbo 46.6 g; 83.8% Cal from Carbo; Fiber 6.3 g; Prot 8 g; 14.4% Cal from Prot

Broccoli and Cheese Soup

1 (15-ounce) jar Cheez Whiz
2 (10-ounce) cans cream of celery soup
2 cups half-and-half
1 (10-ounce) package frozen chopped broccoli

Combine the Cheez Whiz, soup, half-and-half and broccoli in a slow cooker and mix well. Cook, covered, on Low for 8 to 10 hours or on High for 3 to 4 hours. Ladle into soup bowls.

Note: You may double the recipe to fill the slow cooker.

Yield: 6 servings

Nutrients Per Serving: Cal 384; Cal from Fat 255; T Fat 28.4 g; Saturated Fat 16.1 g; 66.4% Cal from Fat; Chol 95 mg; Sod 1921 mg; T Carbo 18.8 g; 19.6% Cal from Carbo; Fiber 2 g; Prot 13.5 g; 14.1% Cal from Prot

Potato Soup

1/2 cup chopped onion
2 tablespoons margarine or butter
3 cups chopped peeled potatoes
1 cup thinly sliced celery
1/2 cup finely chopped carrots
2 tablespoons chopped parsley
1 (10-ounce) can chicken broth
3/4 teaspoon salt
1/8 teaspoon pepper
31/2 cups milk
1 tablespoon chopped pimento (optional)
1/2 cup milk
1/4 cup all-purpose flour

Cook the onion in the margarine in a 3-quart saucepan for 5 minutes or until the onion is tender. Stir in the potatoes, celery, carrots, parsley, broth, salt and pepper. Simmer, covered, for 15 minutes or until the vegetables are tender. Reduce the heat and stir in 31/2 cups milk and the pimento.

Cook until heated through; do not boil. Whisk 1/2 cup milk and the flour in a bowl until blended. Stir into the soup and cook until slightly thickened and bubbly. Ladle into soup bowls.

Yield: 6 servings

Nutrients Per Serving: Cal 230; Cal from Fat 68; T Fat 7.6 g; Saturated Fat 2.7 g; 29.5% Cal from Fat; Chol 13 mg; Sod 742 mg; T Carbo 30.9 g; 53.6% Cal from Carbo; Fiber 2.3 g; Prot 9.7 g; 16.8% Cal from Prot

Baked Potato Soup

2/3 cup butter
2/3 cup all-purpose flour
7 cups milk
4 large baking potatoes, baked,
    peeled and coarsely chopped
4 green onions, chopped

12 slices bacon, crisp-cooked
    and crumbled
1 cup sour cream
1 1/4 cups (5 ounces) shredded
    Cheddar cheese
Salt and pepper to taste

Melt the butter in a large saucepan and stir in the flour. Cook until smooth and bubbly, stirring constantly. Add the milk gradually, stirring constantly. Cook until thickened, stirring frequently. Stir in the potatoes and green onions and bring to a boil. Reduce the heat to low.

Simmer for 10 minutes and stir in the bacon, sour cream, cheese, salt and pepper. Cook until the cheese melts, stirring frequently. Serve in bread bowls or with corn bread.

Yield: 8 servings

Nutrients Per Serving: Cal 573; Cal from Fat 344; T Fat 38.1 g; Saturated Fat 22.5 g; 60.1% Cal from Fat; Chol 102 mg; Sod 599 mg; T Carbo 37.3 g; 26% Cal from Carbo; Fiber 2.4 g; Prot 19.9 g; 13.9% Cal from Prot

Simple Soup

1 (19-ounce) can minestrone soup
1 (15-ounce) can white corn, drained
1 (15-ounce) can mixed vegetables,
    drained

1 (15-ounce) can black beans, drained
1 (15-ounce) can diced tomatoes

Combine the soup, corn, mixed vegetables, beans and tomatoes in a saucepan and mix well. Bring to a boil, stirring occasionally. Ladle into soup bowls.

Yield: 10 servings

Nutrients Per Serving: Cal 138; Cal from Fat 14; T Fat 1.4 g; Saturated Fat 0.4 g; 10.1% Cal from Fat; Chol 1 mg; Sod 632 mg; T Carbo 25.2 g; 73% Cal from Carbo; Fiber 6.9 g; Prot 5.8 g; 16.8% Cal from Prot

Pineapple and Almond Salad

Vinaigrette

1/4 cup vegetable oil
2 tablespoons apple cider vinegar
2 tablespoons sugar
1/4 teaspoon salt
1/8 teaspoon pepper

Salad

1/4 cup slivered almonds
1 tablespoon sugar
1 (8-ounce) can pineapple chunks, drained
1/4 head iceburg lettuce, torn into bite-size pieces
1/4 head romaine, torn into bite-size pieces
2 ribs celery, sliced
2 green onions, sliced

To prepare the vinaigrette, combine the oil, vinegar, sugar, salt and pepper in a jar with a tight-fitting lid and seal tightly. Shake to combine. Chill in the refrigerator.

To prepare the salad, toss the almonds and sugar in a small skillet. Cook over low heat until the almonds are golden brown, stirring frequently. Remove to a plate to cool. Toss the almonds, pineapple, lettuce, celery and green onions in a salad bowl. Add the chilled vinaigrette to the salad just before serving and toss to coat.

Note: The amount of pineapple may be increased according to taste.

Yield: 4 servings

 Nutrients Per Serving: Cal 267; Cal from Fat 169; T Fat 18.8 g; Saturated Fat 2.2 g; 63.4% Cal from Fat; Chol 0 mg; Sod 207 mg; T Carbo 20.6 g; 30.9% Cal from Carbo; Fiber 3.7 g; Prot 3.8 g; 5.7% Cal from Prot

Green Bean, Walnut and Feta Cheese Salad

Walnut Vinaigrette
1 cup walnuts, coarsely chopped
3/4 cup olive oil
1/4 cup white wine vinegar
1 tablespoon chopped fresh dill weed
1/2 teaspoon minced garlic
1/4 teaspoon salt
1/4 teaspoon pepper

Salad
11/2 pounds green beans, trimmed
1 small red onion, thinly sliced
4 ounces feta cheese, crumbled

To prepare the vinaigrette, whisk the walnuts, olive oil, vinegar, dill weed, garlic, salt and pepper in a bowl until combined.

To prepare the salad, steam the beans until tender-crisp; drain. Let cool slightly. Toss the beans, onion and cheese in a bowl. Add the vinaigrette and toss to coat. Marinate, covered, in the refrigerator for 1 hour, stirring occasionally. Serve chilled.

Yield: 6 servings

 Nutrients Per Serving: Cal 480; Cal from Fat 386; T Fat 42.9 g; Saturated Fat 7.2 g; 80.4% Cal from Fat; Chol 17 mg; Sod 319 mg; T Carbo 13.4 g; 11.2% Cal from Carbo; Fiber 5.3 g; Prot 10.1 g; 8.4% Cal from Prot

Creamy Buttermilk Coleslaw

1 pound red or green cabbage, finely shredded
1 teaspoon salt
1 carrot, shredded
1/2 cup buttermilk
2 tablespoons mayonnaise
2 tablespoons sour cream
2 tablespoons chopped fresh parsley
1 small shallot, minced
1/2 teaspoon cider vinegar
1/2 teaspoon sugar
1/4 teaspoon Dijon mustard
1/4 teaspoon salt
1/8 teaspoon pepper

Toss the cabbage with 1 teaspoon salt in a bowl. Place in a colander and let stand for 1 to 4 hours or until the cabbage wilts. Rinse with cold water and gently press the cabbage to remove any excess moisture. Pat dry with paper towels.

Toss the cabbage and carrot in a bowl. Mix the buttermilk, mayonnaise, sour cream, parsley, shallot, vinegar, sugar, Dijon mustard, salt and pepper in a bowl. Add to the cabbage mixture and toss to coat. Chill, covered, for 30 minutes or longer before serving.

Yield: 6 servings

 Nutrients Per Serving: Cal 82; Cal from Fat 45; T Fat 4.9 g; Saturated Fat 1.2 g; 55% Cal from Fat; Chol 5 mg; Sod 467 mg; T Carbo 7.1 g; 34.7% Cal from Carbo; Fiber 2.1 g; Prot 2.1 g; 10.3% Cal from Prot

Overnight Slaw

1 head cabbage, shredded
1 teaspoon salt
1 green bell pepper, finely chopped
1 carrot, grated
2 cups sugar
1 cup vinegar
1 teaspoon whole mustard seeds

Toss the cabbage with the salt in a bowl. Place in a colander and let stand for 1 hour. Press the excess moisture from the cabbage. Mix the cabbage, bell pepper and carrot in a heatproof bowl.

Combine the sugar, vinegar and mustard seeds in a saucepan. Cook until the sugar dissolves, stirring constantly. Pour over the cabbage mixture and toss to coat. Chill, covered, overnight.

Note: Leftovers may be frozen for future use.

Yield: 8 servings

 Nutrients Per Serving: Cal 286; Cal from Fat 7; T Fat 0.7 g; Saturated Fat 0.1 g; 2.4% Cal from Fat; Chol 0 mg; Sod 339 mg; T Carbo 66.1 g; 92.5% Cal from Carbo; Fiber 5.8 g; Prot 3.6 g; 5% Cal from Prot

TRY SUBSTITUTING BROCCOLI FOR THE AVOCADO
IN THE COBB SALAD (PAGE 71). A TENDER-CRISP BROCCOLI IS
A COLORFUL SUBSTITUTION.

Cobb Salad

Dijon Vinaigrette
1/2 cup extra-virgin olive oil
2 tablespoons red wine vinegar
2 teaspoons fresh lemon juice
1 teaspoon Worcestershire sauce
1 teaspoon Dijon mustard
1 garlic clove, minced
1/2 teaspoon salt
1/4 teaspoon sugar
1/8 teaspoon pepper

Salad
8 slices bacon, cut into 1/4-inch pieces
3 (8-ounce) boneless skinless
    chicken breasts
Salt and pepper to taste
12 cups (bite-size pieces) lettuce
1 pint grape tomatoes, cut into halves
3 hard-boiled eggs, sliced or
    cut into wedges
2 avocados, cut into 1/2-inch pieces
2 ounces blue cheese, crumbled
3 tablespoons minced fresh chives

To prepare the vinaigrette, whisk the olive oil, vinegar, lemon juice, Worcestershire sauce, Dijon mustard, garlic, salt, sugar and pepper in a bowl until combined.

You may prepare up to one day in advance and store, covered, in the refrigerator. Bring to room temperature before serving.

To prepare the salad, cook the bacon in a skillet until crisp and remove to paper towels to drain. Season the chicken with salt and pepper. Arrange the chicken in a single layer on a broiler rack sprayed with nonstick cooking spray. Arrange the broiler rack in a broiler pan and broil 6 inches from the heat source for 4 to 8 minutes or until light brown. Turn the chicken and broil for 6 to 8 minutes longer or until cooked through or until a meat thermometer registers 165 degrees. Let stand until cool and cut into 1/2-inch pieces.

Toss the lettuce with 5 tablespoons of the vinaigrette in bowl to coat. Line a large serving platter with the lettuce. Toss the chicken with 1/2 cup of the remaining vinaigrette in a bowl and arrange the chicken along one edge of the platter. Toss the tomatoes with 1 tablespoon of the remaining vinaigrette in a bowl and arrange the tomatoes in a row opposite the chicken. Arrange the eggs and avocados in separate rows near the center of the platter. Drizzle with the remaining vinaigrette and sprinkle the salad evenly with the bacon, cheese and chives. Serve immediately.

Yield: 8 servings

Photograph on the cover

Nutrients Per Serving: Cal 495; Cal from Fat 408; T Fat 45.5 g; Saturated Fat 12.7 g; 82.4% Cal from Fat; Chol 125 mg; Sod 582 mg; T Carbo 6.4 g; 5.2% Cal from Carbo; Fiber 3.6 g; Prot 15.4 g; 12.4% Cal from Prot

German Potato Salad

2 pounds small to medium
   red potatoes
1 tablespoon salt
8 ounces bacon, cut horizontally into
   1/2-inch pieces
1 onion, finely chopped (1 cup)
1/2 teaspoon sugar

1/2 cup white vinegar
1 tablespoon German-style whole
   grain mustard
1/4 teaspoon pepper
1/4 cup fresh Italian parsley
   leaves, chopped
Salt to taste

Cut the small potatoes into halves and the medium potatoes into quarters. Combine the potatoes and 1 tablespoon salt with enough water to cover in a large saucepan. Bring to a boil over high heat and reduce the heat to medium. Simmer for 10 minutes or until the potatoes are tender. Drain, reserving the potatoes and 1/2 cup of the cooking liquid. Return the potatoes to the saucepan and cover to keep warm.

Cook the bacon in a large skillet over medium heat for 5 minutes or until crisp. Remove the bacon using a slotted spoon to a plate lined with paper towels to drain, reserving 1/4 cup of the bacon drippings. Cook the onion in the reserved bacon drippings over medium heat for 4 minutes or just until the onion is tender and begins to brown, stirring occasionally. Stir in the sugar and cook for 30 seconds or until the sugar dissolves, stirring constantly. Add the reserved cooking liquid and vinegar and bring to a simmer.

Simmer for 3 minutes or until the liquid is reduced to about 1 cup, stirring frequently. Remove from the heat and whisk in the mustard and pepper. Add the potatoes, bacon and parsley and toss to combine. Taste and adjust with salt to taste. Spoon the potato salad into a serving bowl and serve immediately.

Yield: 8 servings

 Nutrients Per Serving: Cal 277; Cal from Fat 163; T Fat 18.1 g; Saturated Fat 6.2 g; 58.8% Cal from Fat; Chol 19 mg; Sod 1100 mg; T Carbo 23.4 g; 33.8% Cal from Carbo; Fiber 2.3 g; Prot 5.1 g; 7.4% Cal from Prot

Spinach Salad with Warm Bacon Dressing

3 eggs

4 cups ice water

6 ounces baby spinach (about 8 cups)

3 tablespoons cider vinegar

1/2 teaspoon sugar

1/4 teaspoon pepper

1/16 teaspoon salt

10 ounces thick-cut bacon, cut into
    1/2-inch pieces

1/2 red onion, coarsely chopped
    (1/2 cup)

1 small garlic clove, minced or
    pressed (1/2 teaspoon)

Place the eggs in a medium saucepan and add enough water to cover by 1 inch. Bring to a boil over high heat and remove from the heat. Let stand, covered, for 10 minutes. Fill a medium bowl with the ice water. Remove the eggs to the ice water using a slotted spoon and let stand for 5 minutes; drain. Peel the eggs and slice each egg lengthwise into quarters.

Place the spinach in a large heatproof bowl. Whisk the vinegar, sugar, pepper and salt in a bowl until the sugar dissolves. Cook the bacon in a skillet over medium-high heat for 10 minutes or until crisp, stirring occasionally. Remove the bacon using a slotted spoon to paper towels to drain, reserving 3 tablespoons of the bacon drippings.

Cook the onion in the reserved bacon drippings over medium heat for 3 minutes or until slightly softened. Stir in the garlic and cook for 15 seconds or until fragrant. Mix in the vinegar mixture and remove from the heat. Scrape the bottom of the skillet with a wooden spoon to loosen any brown bits. Pour the hot vinegar dressing over the spinach. Add the bacon and toss gently with tongs until the spinach is slightly wilted. Divide the spinach mixture evenly among six salad plates and top each salad with two egg quarters. Serve immediately.

Yield: 6 servings

 Nutrients Per Serving: Cal 333; Cal from Fat 285; T Fat 31.8 g; Saturated Fat 11.6 g; 85.7% Cal from Fat; Chol 138 mg; Sod 423 mg; T Carbo 3.4 g; 4.1% Cal from Carbo; Fiber 1.1 g; Prot 8.5 g; 10.2% Cal from Prot

Spinach Salad with Spicy Honey Dressing

Spicy Honey Dressing
1/2 cup vegetable oil
1/4 cup honey
1/4 cup vinegar
1/4 cup chopped onion
1 1/2 teaspoons Worcestershire sauce
3 tablespoons chili sauce
1/4 teaspoon salt

Salad
4 cups fresh spinach leaves, trimmed
   and torn

1 cup fresh parsley, minced
1 cup mushrooms, sliced
2 tomatoes, cut into wedges
2 ribs celery, chopped
1 cup canned bean sprouts, drained
   and rinsed
1 1/2 cups (6 ounces) shredded
   Cheddar cheese
1 cup salted sunflower kernels
1/4 teaspoon salt
1/4 teaspoon pepper
1/4 teaspoon garlic salt

To prepare the dressing, combine the oil, honey, vinegar, onion, Worcestershire sauce, chili sauce and salt in a jar with a tight-fitting lid and seal tightly. Shake to mix. Store any leftover dressing in the refrigerator.

To prepare the salad, toss the spinach, parsley, mushrooms, tomatoes, celery, bean sprouts, cheese, sunflower kernels, salt, pepper and garlic salt in a large salad bowl. Drizzle with the desired amount of the dressing and toss to coat. Serve immediately.

Yield: 12 servings

Nutrients Per Serving: Cal 192; Cal from Fat 128; T Fat 14.2 g; Saturated Fat 4.2 g; 66.8% Cal from Fat; Chol 15 mg; Sod 428 mg; T Carbo 10.9 g; 22.8% Cal from Carbo; Fiber 1.5 g; Prot 5 g; 10.4% Cal from Prot. *Nutritional profile includes the entire amount of the dressing.*

Tomato Salad

Juice of 2 limes
1/2 teaspoon sugar
Salt and pepper to taste
2 red onions, chopped
4 firm tomatoes, finely chopped
1/2 cucumber, finely chopped
1 green chile pepper, finely chopped
Chopped cilantro leaves to taste
Fresh mint leaves for garnish

Combine the lime juice, sugar, salt and pepper in a glass salad bowl and mix well. Let stand until the sugar and salt dissolve, stirring occasionally. Add the onions, tomatoes, cucumber, chile pepper and cilantro and mix well. Garnish with mint leaves just before serving.

Yield: 6 servings

Nutrients Per Serving: Cal 52; Cal from Fat 1; T Fat 0.1 g; Saturated Fat 0 g; 1.9% Cal from Fat; Chol 0 mg; Sod 5 mg; T Carbo 10.9 g; 84.2% Cal from Carbo; Fiber 2.1 g; Prot 1.8 g; 13.9% Cal from Prot

Yogurt Salad

1¹/2 cups plain low-fat natural yogurt
2 teaspoons honey
1¹/2 cups finely shredded cabbage
16 white grapes, cut into halves
2 carrots, thickly sliced
2 green onions, coarsely chopped

¹/2 cup cashews
¹/3 cup golden raisins
1 teaspoon chopped fresh mint
¹/2 teaspoon salt
3 or 4 sprigs of mint for garnish

Mix the yogurt and honey in a bowl with a fork. Combine the cabbage, grape halves, carrots, green onions, cashews, raisins, 1 teaspoon mint and the salt in a bowl and mix well. Add the yogurt mixture to the cabbage mixture and mix to coat. Spoon the salad into a serving bowl and garnish with the mint sprigs. Serve immediately.

Yield: 4 servings

Nutrients Per Serving: Cal 265; Cal from Fat 87; T Fat 9.5 g; Saturated Fat 2.4 g; 32.9% Cal from Fat; Chol 6 mg; Sod 387 mg; T Carbo 35.6 g; 53.8% Cal from Carbo; Fiber 3.8 g; Prot 8.8 g; 13.3% Cal from Prot

Spaghetti Salad

16 ounces spaghetti
4 ounces sharp Cheddar
    cheese, cubed
¹/2 cup chopped cherry tomatoes
¹/2 cup chopped onion
¹/2 cup chopped cauliflower

¹/2 cup chopped broccoli
¹/2 cup chopped cucumber
3 tablespoons Salad Supreme
    seasoning
1 (24-ounce) bottle Zesty Italian
    salad dressing

Combine the pasta with enough water to cover in a saucepan and cook until al dente; drain. Rinse the pasta with cool water and drain again. Toss the pasta, cheese, tomatoes, onion, cauliflower, broccoli and cucumber in a large bowl and sprinkle with the seasoning. Add the salad dressing and mix to coat.

Yield: 8 servings

Nutrients Per Serving: Cal 680; Cal from Fat 420; T Fat 46.7 g; Saturated Fat 9.1 g; 61.8% Cal from Fat; Chol 15 mg; Sod 765 mg; T Carbo 53.1 g; 31.3% Cal from Carbo; Fiber 2.1 g; Prot 11.8 g; 6.9% Cal from Prot. *Nutritional profile does not include Salad Supreme seasoning.*

Pasta Salad with Pesto and Peas

Basil Pesto
1 tablespoon chopped walnuts
1 tablespoon pine nuts
2 garlic cloves, minced
1 1/4 cups packed fresh
    basil leaves
1/4 teaspoon kosher salt
1/4 teaspoon pepper
6 tablespoons extra-virgin olive oil
1/4 cup (1 ounce) grated
    Parmesan cheese

Salad
2/3 (10-ounce) package frozen chopped
    spinach, thawed and drained
8 ounces fusilli
8 ounces bow-tie pasta
Salt to taste
2 1/2 tablespoons extra-virgin olive oil
2 tablespoons fresh lemon juice
3/4 cup mayonnaise
1 cup frozen peas, thawed
6 tablespoons grated Parmesan cheese
1/4 cup pine nuts
1/2 teaspoon kosher salt
1/2 teaspoon pepper

To prepare the pesto, combine the walnuts, pine nuts and garlic in a food processor fitted with a steel blade. Process for 30 seconds. Add the basil, salt and pepper. Add the olive oil gradually, processing constantly until puréed. Add the cheese and process for 1 minute longer.

To prepare the salad, press the excess moisture from the spinach. Cook the pasta in boiling salted water in a saucepan for 10 to 12 minutes or until al dente; drain. Toss the pasta with the olive oil in a large bowl and let stand until cool.

Combine the pesto, spinach and lemon juice in a food processor fitted with a steel blade and process until puréed. Add the mayonnaise and process until blended. Add the pesto mixture to the pasta and toss to coat. Stir in the peas, cheese, pine nuts, salt and pepper. Serve at room temperature.

Yield: 8 servings

 Nutrients Per Serving: Cal 568; Cal from Fat 326; T Fat 36.2 g; Saturated Fat 6.2 g; 57.4% Cal from Fat; Chol 14 mg; Sod 537 mg; T Carbo 46.9 g; 33.1% Cal from Carbo; Fiber 3.9 g; Prot 13.5 g; 9.5% Cal from Prot

Pasta Salad with Sun-Dried Tomato Vinaigrette

Sun-Dried Tomato Vinaigrette
5 oil-pack sun-dried tomatoes, drained
6 tablespoons extra-virgin olive oil
2 tablespoons red wine vinegar
1 garlic clove, minced
2 teaspoons kosher salt
1 teaspoon capers, drained
3/4 teaspoon pepper

Salad
8 ounces fusilli
Salt to taste
12 ounces baby eggplant, peeled and
    cut into 1/2-inch pieces

1/2 teaspoon kosher salt
1 tablespoon olive oil
1 tablespoon brown sugar
16 ounces mozzarella cheese, cut into
    1/2-inch cubes
1 pint grape tomatoes, cut into halves
6 oil-pack sun-dried tomatoes,
    drained and chopped
1 cup (4 ounces) grated
    Parmesan cheese
1 cup packed fresh basil
    leaves, julienned

To prepare the vinaigrette, process the sun-dried tomatoes, olive oil, vinegar, garlic, salt, capers and pepper in a food processor fitted with a steel blade until almost smooth.

To prepare the salad, cook the pasta in boiling salted water in a saucepan for 12 minutes. Drain and let stand until cool. Place the eggplant in a colander and sprinkle with 1/2 teaspoon kosher salt. Let stand for 30 minutes. Press the eggplant gently to release any excess moisture and pat dry with paper towels.

Heat the olive oil in a saucepan over medium-high heat and add the eggplant and brown sugar. Cook for 6 minutes or until the eggplant is light brown, stirring frequently. Toss the pasta, eggplant, mozzarella cheese, grape tomatoes and sun-dried tomatoes in a large bowl. Add the vinaigrette and mix to coat. Sprinkle with the Parmesan cheese and basil and toss to combine.

Yield: 8 servings

 Nutrients Per Serving: Cal 521; Cal from Fat 291; T Fat 32.4 g; Saturated Fat 12.1 g; 55.9% Cal from Fat; Chol 55 mg; Sod 800 mg; T Carbo 35.5 g; 27.3% Cal from Carbo; Fiber 4.4 g; Prot 21.9 g; 16.8% Cal from Prot

Curried Rice Salad

16 cups water
1¹/2 cups long grain rice
1¹/2 teaspoons salt
2 tablespoons vegetable oil
2 cups cauliflower florets
1 tablespoon curry powder
¹/2 teaspoon salt

¹/4 cup raisins
¹/4 cup water
¹/2 cup toasted cashews
1 mango, finely chopped
3 tablespoons minced chives
¹/2 teaspoon salt
¹/4 teaspoon pepper

Bring 16 cups water to a boil in a large stockpot. Heat a medium skillet over medium heat for 3 minutes or until hot and add the rice. Cook for 5 minutes or until some of the grains turn opaque, stirring frequently. Add 1¹/2 teaspoons salt and the rice to the boiling water and return to a boil. Cook for 8 to 10 minutes or until the rice is tender; drain. Spread the rice on a rimmed baking sheet lined with foil. Let stand until cool.

Heat the oil in a medium skillet over high heat until shimmering. Stir in the cauliflower, curry powder and ¹/2 teaspoon salt. Cook for 1 minute or until fragrant, stirring constantly. Stir in the raisins and ¹/4 cup water. Reduce the heat to medium-high and cook for 3 minutes or until the water evaporates and the cauliflower is tender.

Remove the cauliflower mixture to a large bowl and stir in the rice, cashews, mango, chives, ¹/2 teaspoon salt and the pepper. Let stand for 20 minutes to allow the flavors to blend and serve.

Yield: 8 servings

Nutrients Per Serving: Cal 135; Cal from Fat 68; T Fat 7.6 g; Saturated Fat 1.2 g; 50.4% Cal from Fat; Chol 0 mg; Sod 746 mg; T Carbo 14.3 g; 42.4% Cal from Carbo; Fiber 1.9 g; Prot 2.4 g; 7.1% Cal from Prot

Tabouli

3 cups water
3/4 teaspoon salt
1 1/2 cups bulgur wheat
2 tomatoes, chopped
1/2 cup cooked white beans
1/4 to 1/2 cup fresh parsley, chopped
Juice of 2 lemons
3 tablespoons olive oil
1 garlic clove, minced
1 tablespoon chopped fresh mint
Pepper to taste

Bring the water and salt to a boil in a saucepan and stir in the wheat. Return to a boil and remove from the heat. Let stand, covered, for 15 minutes. Chill, covered, in the refrigerator; drain. Stir in the tomatoes, beans, parsley, lemon juice, olive oil, garlic, mint and pepper. Taste and adjust the seasonings.

Yield: 8 servings

Nutrients Per Serving: Cal 101; Cal from Fat 47; T Fat 5.2 g; Saturated Fat 0.7 g; 46.7% Cal from Fat; Chol 0 mg; Sod 226 mg; T Carbo 10.8 g; 42.9% Cal from Carbo; Fiber 1.1 g; Prot 2.6 g; 10.3% Cal from Prot

Vegetables & Sides

Diverticular Disease

Diverticular disease occurs when small out-pouches or sacs, called diverticula, develop along the inner lining of the gastrointestinal tract. **Diverticulosis** refers to the presence of diverticula and is especially common in Americans over the age of sixty. Many individuals with diverticulosis experience no symptoms. Diverticulosis is usually discovered during a colonoscopy or radiographic study.

    Diverticulitis is an inflammation or infection of one of the diverticula. Diverticulitis is associated with fever, abdominal pain, diarrhea, and/or constipation and decreased appetite. Treatment for diverticulitis may range from antibiotics to, in rare cases, surgery.

    Frequently patients ask, "What causes diverticulosis?" There are many theories as to the cause of diverticula. One of the most accepted theories is one of abnormal contraction of the colon muscles. This results in high pressure, which pushes against the colon wall and causes diverticula to form in weak spots along the colon wall. Constipation, a major cause of increased intra-colonic pressure, should be avoided. A diet high in fiber may improve the symptoms of constipation and decrease chances of developing diverticulosis.

Baked Artichoke Frittata

1 cup canned or thawed frozen chopped artichoke hearts
1 cup (4 ounces) shredded white Cheddar cheese
6 eggs
1/4 cup milk
1/4 cup half-and-half
1/4 teaspoon salt
1/8 teaspoon pepper
1/8 teaspoon nutmeg
1/4 cup (1 ounce) grated Parmesan cheese

Divide the artichokes evenly among four individual baking dishes or ramekins. Sprinkle 1/4 cup of the Cheddar cheese over the top of each.

Beat the eggs, milk, half-and-half, salt, pepper and nutmeg in a mixing bowl until blended and pour over the prepared layers. Sprinkle with the Parmesan cheese and bake at 350 degrees for 20 minutes. Serve immediately.

Yield: 4 servings

 Nutrients Per Serving: Cal 300; Cal from Fat 188; T Fat 20.7 g; Saturated Fat 10.8 g; 62.7% Cal from Fat; Chol 358 mg; Sod 713 mg; T Carbo 6.8 g; 9.1% Cal from Carbo; Fiber 0.9 g; Prot 21.2 g; 28.3% Cal from Prot

OVERCOOKING VEGETABLES CAN REMOVE CANCER-FIGHTING VITAMINS, MINERALS, AND NUTRIENTS. VEGETABLES COOKED IN THE MICROWAVE RETAIN 80 TO 100 PERCENT OF THEIR NUTRIENTS.

Creamy Asparagus Bake

1¹/2 pounds trimmed asparagus spears
1 tablespoon butter
1 tablespoon all-purpose flour
1 cup half-and-half
¹/2 teaspoon chicken bouillon granules
¹/8 teaspoon nutmeg
¹/8 teaspoon salt
¹/2 cup (2 ounces) shredded Swiss cheese
2 tablespoons crushed butter crackers

Cook the asparagus in a small amount of water in a skillet for 6 to 8 minutes or until tender-crisp; drain. Arrange the asparagus in a greased 9×13-inch baking dish. Cover to keep warm.

Melt the butter in a small saucepan over low heat and stir in the flour. Cook for 1 minute, stirring constantly. Whisk in the half-and-half, bouillon granules, nutmeg and salt. Bring to a boil over medium heat and cook for 2 minutes, stirring constantly. Remove from the heat and stir in the cheese.

Pour the cheese sauce over the asparagus and sprinkle with the cracker crumbs. Broil 6 inches from the heat source for 3 to 5 minutes or until light brown. Serve immediately.

Yield: 12 servings

Nutrients Per Serving: Cal 79; Cal from Fat 46; T Fat 5.1 g; Saturated Fat 3 g; 58.4% Cal from Fat; Chol 15 mg; Sod 64 mg; T Carbo 4.6 g; 23.4% Cal from Carbo; Fiber 1.2 g; Prot 3.6 g; 18.3% Cal from Prot

Baked Beans

2 (20-ounce) cans pork and beans
1 (15-ounce) can black beans, drained
1 (15-ounce) can butter beans or
    cooked dried lima beans, drained
1 (15-ounce) can chunky tomatoes with
    green peppers and onions
3/4 cup packed brown sugar
5 slices bacon, crisp-cooked and crumbled, or
    1/2 cup bacon bits
1/2 (8-ounce) bottle barbecue sauce
1/2 cup ketchup
1/2 cup mustard
2 tablespoons minced onion
Salt and pepper to taste

Combine all the beans in a slow cooker. Stir in the tomatoes, brown sugar, bacon, barbecue sauce, ketchup, mustard, onion, salt and pepper. Cook, covered, on Low for 8 to 10 hours or to the desired consistency, or bake in a baking dish at 350 degrees for 45 to 60 minutes.

Yield: 12 servings

Nutrients Per Serving: Cal 356; Cal from Fat 110; T Fat 12.4 g; Saturated Fat 2.1 g; 30.9% Cal from Fat; Chol 10 mg; Sod 917 mg; T Carbo 51.2 g; 57.6% Cal from Carbo; Fiber 9.1 g; Prot 10.2 g; 11.5% Cal from Prot

Broccoli and Rice

1 onion, finely chopped
1 tablespoon butter
1/2 teaspoon dry mustard
8 ounces processed Cheddar cheese or
  Cheez Whiz
1 (10-ounce) can cream of mushroom soup
3 cups cooked rice (1 cup dry)
1 (10-ounce) package frozen broccoli
1 (3-ounce) can French-fried onions

Cook the onion in the butter in a medium saucepan and then stir in the dry mustard. Mix in the cheese and gradually stir in the soup. Add the rice and broccoli and mix gently. Spoon into a shallow baking dish and sprinkle with the French-fried onions. Bake at 350 degrees for 20 minutes or until bubbly. Serve immediately.

Yield: 8 servings

Nutrients Per Serving: Cal 333; Cal from Fat 171; T Fat 18.9 g; Saturated Fat 9.9 g; 51.3% Cal from Fat; Chol 34 mg; Sod 538 mg; T Carbo 30 g; 36% Cal from Carbo; Fiber 2 g; Prot 10.6 g; 12.7% Cal from Prot

Broccoli, Carrots and Rice

1 cup long, medium or short grain rice
1 (10-ounce) package frozen broccoli,
    cut into bite-size pieces
1/2 cup boiling water
Salt to taste
2 carrots, sliced
1/2 cup boiling water
2 tablespoons olive oil
1 tablespoon butter or margarine
2 garlic cloves, minced or pressed
1/2 cup (2 ounces) grated Parmesan cheese
1/4 teaspoon cracked pepper

Cook the rice using the package directions. Combine the broccoli, 1/2 cup boiling water and salt in a saucepan and cook for 5 minutes or until the broccoli is tender; drain. Combine the carrots, 1/2 cup boiling water and salt in a saucepan and cook for 6 to 8 minutes or until the carrots are tender; drain. Heat the olive oil, butter and garlic in a saucepan until hot.

Combine the rice, broccoli and carrots in a bowl and mix well. Add the garlic mixture, cheese and pepper and toss to mix. Add additional Parmesan cheese, if desired.

Yield: 6 servings

 Nutrients Per Serving: Cal 235; Cal from Fat 86; T Fat 9.5 g; Saturated Fat 2.7 g; 36.6% Cal from Fat; Chol 7 mg; Sod 217 mg; T Carbo 29.8 g; 50.7% Cal from Carbo; Fiber 2.4 g; Prot 7.5 g; 12.8% Cal from Prot

Breaded Cauliflower

Florets of 1 small head cauliflower (5 cups)
4 egg yolks
1 teaspoon garlic powder
1 teaspoon onion powder
1 teaspoon minced fresh parsley
1/2 teaspoon sugar
1/2 teaspoon salt
1/4 teaspoon pepper
1 cup seasoned bread crumbs
3 tablespoons grated Parmesan cheese
3/4 cup (11/2 sticks) butter or margarine
Chopped fresh parsley for garnish

Combine the cauliflower with a small amount of water in a skillet and bring to a boil. Reduce the heat to low and simmer, covered, for 8 minutes or until the cauliflower is tender-crisp; drain. Whisk the egg yolks, garlic powder, onion powder, 1 teaspoon parsley, the sugar, salt and pepper in a bowl until combined. Mix the bread crumbs and cheese in a large sealable plastic bag.

Dip the cauliflower florets in batches in the egg mixture and then coat with the bread crumb mixture. Melt the butter in a skillet over medium-high heat. Add the coated cauliflower in batches and cook for 4 minutes or until golden brown; drain. Garnish with chopped parsley.

Yield: 6 servings

Nutrients Per Serving: Cal 360; Cal from Fat 250; T Fat 27.7 g; Saturated Fat 16.1 g; 69.4% Cal from Fat; Chol 194 mg; Sod 1047 mg; T Carbo 19.7 g; 21.9% Cal from Carbo; Fiber 2.9 g; Prot 7.8 g; 8.7% Cal from Prot

Roasted Cauliflower

1 (2-pound) head cauliflower
1/4 cup extra-virgin olive oil

Kosher salt and pepper
to taste

Cut the stem even with the bottom of the cauliflower head and discard any leaves. Cut the head into eight wedges. Brush each wedge with 1 1/2 teaspoons of the olive oil and sprinkle with salt and pepper. Arrange the wedges cut side down on a 10×15-inch baking pan lined with foil.

Bake, tightly covered with foil, at 475 degrees for 10 minutes. Remove the foil and bake for 10 minutes. Turn the wedges and bake for 10 minutes longer. Serve immediately.

Note: For variety, add 2 teaspoons curry, ginger, garlic powder or chili powder to the olive oil.

Yield: 4 servings

 Nutrients Per Serving: Cal 191; Cal from Fat 126; T Fat 14 g; Saturated Fat 1.9 g; 65.9% Cal from Fat; Chol 0 mg; Sod 68 mg; T Carbo 11.8 g; 24.7% Cal from Carbo; Fiber 5.7 g; Prot 4.5 g; 9.4% Cal from Prot

Corn and Broccoli Bake

1 (8-ounce) package Chicken in a
   Biskit crackers, crushed
1/2 cup (1 stick) butter or
   margarine, melted
1 (14-ounce) can cream-style corn

1 (15-ounce) can whole kernel
   corn, drained
1 (10-ounce) package frozen chopped
   broccoli, thawed

Toss the cracker crumbs and butter in a bowl until coated. Reserve 1/2 cup of the crumb mixture for the topping. Combine the corn, broccoli and remaining crumb mixture in a bowl and mix well. Spoon into a greased 2-quart baking dish and sprinkle with the reserved crumb mixture. Bake at 375 degrees for 25 to 30 minutes or until light brown. Serve immediately.

Yield: 8 servings

 Nutrients Per Serving: Cal 347; Cal from Fat 174; T Fat 19.3 g; Saturated Fat 3.5 g; 50.1% Cal from Fat; Chol 0 mg; Sod 729 mg; T Carbo 38.1 g; 43.9% Cal from Carbo; Fiber 2.8 g; Prot 5.2 g; 6% Cal from Prot

Baked Corn

1/2 cup (1 stick) margarine
1 (15-ounce) can whole kernel corn
1 (14-ounce) can cream-style corn
1 (8-ounce) package corn muffin mix

1 cup sour cream or low-fat
   sour cream
3 eggs, lightly beaten
1 tablespoon sugar

Melt the margarine in a 9×12-inch baking dish. Combine the corn, muffin mix, sour cream, eggs and sugar in a bowl and mix well. Spread in the prepared baking dish and bake at 350 degrees for 1 1/4 hours. Serve immediately.

Yield: 8 servings

 Nutrients Per Serving: Cal 405; Cal from Fat 207; T Fat 23.1 g; Saturated Fat 7.9 g; 51.1% Cal from Fat; Chol 92 mg; Sod 711 mg; T Carbo 42.5 g; 42% Cal from Carbo; Fiber 1.7 g; Prot 7 g; 6.9% Cal from Prot

Corn Pudding

1 1/2 cups milk
3 eggs, lightly beaten
6 tablespoons sugar
1/4 cup all-purpose flour

Salt to taste
1 1/2 to 2 pints frozen corn, thawed
3 tablespoons margarine

Whisk the milk and eggs in a bowl until blended. Add the sugar, flour and salt and mix well. Stir in the corn.
Pour into a 7×11-inch baking dish and dot with the margarine. Bake at 300 degrees for 1 hour or until golden brown. You may substitute fresh corn kernels for the frozen.

Yield: 12 servings

 Nutrients Per Serving: Cal 149; Cal from Fat 46; T Fat 5 g; Saturated Fat 1.4 g; 30.8% Cal from Fat; Chol 55 mg; Sod 66 mg; T Carbo 21.3 g; 57.1% Cal from Carbo; Fiber 1.4 g; Prot 4.5 g; 12.1% Cal from Prot

Eggplant with Yogurt (Borani)

1 large eggplant, sliced
Salt to taste
2 tablespoons vegetable oil
1 cup yogurt
2 teaspoons ground cumin

1/2 teaspoon garlic paste
Pepper to taste
3 tablespoons chopped cilantro
    for garnish

Layer the eggplant slices in a colander, sprinkling each layer with salt. Drain for 30 minutes and rinse with cold water. Pat the slices dry with paper towels.

Heat the oil in a large skillet over medium heat and add the eggplant slices. Cook until golden brown on both sides. Remove the eggplant slices to a paper towel to drain and then arrange in a serving dish.

Mix the yogurt, cumin, garlic paste, salt and pepper in a bowl and spoon over the eggplant slices. Garnish with the cilantro and serve immediately with pita bread.

Yield: 4 servings

Nutrients Per Serving: Cal 155; Cal from Fat 75; T Fat 8.2 g; Saturated Fat 1.6 g; 48.3% Cal from Fat; Chol 4 mg; Sod 50 mg; T Carbo 15 g; 38.6% Cal from Carbo; Fiber 4.4 g; Prot 5.1 g; 13.1% Cal from Prot. *Nutritional profile does not include garlic paste.*

WATERMELON IS A RICH SOURCE OF THE CAROTENOID *LYCOPENE*, OFFERING
ABOUT 7.4 MG PER 1 CUP OF FRUIT. WATERMELON HAS ABOUT
60 PERCENT MORE LYCOPENE THAN RAW TOMATOES (COOKED TOMATOES
ARE MORE LYCOPENE RICH).

Sour Cream-Baked Lima Beans

1 pound dried lima beans,
   sorted and rinsed
1 cup sour cream
3/4 cup packed brown sugar

1/2 cup (1 stick) butter, softened
1 tablespoon salt
1 tablespoon dry mustard
1 tablespoon molasses

Cook the lima beans using the package directions. Drain any excess liquid. Mix the sour cream, brown sugar, butter, salt, dry mustard and molasses in a bowl. Stir into the lima beans. Spoon the lima bean mixture into a greased baking dish and bake at 350 degrees for 1 1/2 to 2 hours or until of the desired consistency.

Yield: 6 servings

Nutrients Per Serving: Cal 602; Cal from Fat 215; T Fat 23.8 g; Saturated Fat 14.6 g; 35.7% Cal from Fat; Chol 58 mg; Sod 1398 mg; T Carbo 78.5 g; 52.2% Cal from Carbo; Fiber 30.9 g; Prot 18.2 g; 12.1% Cal from Prot

Vidalia Onion Casserole

1/2 cup (1 stick) butter or margarine
4 Vidalia onions, cut into 1/4-inch
   slices and separated
   into rings
15 saltine crackers, crushed

1 (10-ounce) can cream of
   mushroom soup
2 eggs, beaten
1/2 to 3/4 cup milk
1 cup (4 ounces) shredded sharp
   Cheddar cheese

Melt the butter in a skillet and add the onions. Sauté until the onions are translucent. Reserve 3 tablespoons of the cracker crumbs and sprinkle the remaining cracker crumbs over the bottom of a lightly greased 2-quart baking dish.

Alternate layers of the onions and soup in the prepared baking dish. Mix the eggs and milk in a bowl until blended and pour over the prepared layers. Sprinkle with the cheese and reserved cracker crumbs. Bake at 350 degrees for 30 minutes.

Yield: 8 servings

Nutrients Per Serving: Cal 225; Cal from Fat 148; T Fat 16.3 g; Saturated Fat 8.6 g; 65.8% Cal from Fat; Chol 86 mg; Sod 462 mg; T Carbo 14.9 g; 26.5% Cal from Carbo; Fiber 1.5 g; Prot 4.3 g; 7.7% Cal from Prot

Twice-Baked Potatoes

2 (8-ounce) baking potatoes
2 tablespoons unsalted butter, softened
2/3 cup shredded sharp Cheddar cheese
1/4 cup sour cream
1 tablespoon chopped chives
Salt and pepper to taste
3 slices bacon, crisp-cooked and crumbled

Prick each potato once with a knife and arrange on a baking sheet. Bake for 1 1/4 hours or until the skins are crisp and the potatoes are tender. Cut lengthwise into halves. Scoop the pulp into a bowl, leaving approximately a 3/8-inch shell. Arrange the shells cut side up on a baking sheet.

Mash the pulp with the butter until smooth. Fold in the cheese, sour cream and chives. Add the salt, pepper and bacon and mix gently. Mound the potato mixture evenly into the shells and bake at 400 degrees for 15 minutes or until light brown.

Yield: 4 servings

Nutrients Per Serving: Cal 323; Cal from Fat 209; T Fat 23.2 g; Saturated Fat 12.6 g; 64.8% Cal from Fat; Chol 57 mg; Sod 383 mg; T Carbo 15.1 g; 18.7% Cal from Carbo; Fiber 2.8 g; Prot 13.3 g; 16.5% Cal from Prot

PEOPLE WHO EAT FIVE TO NINE SERVINGS PER DAY OF FRUITS AND
VEGETABLES CAN CUT THEIR RISK OF CANCER BY 50 PERCENT COMPARED TO THOSE
WHO EAT ONE OR LESS SERVINGS PER DAY.

Broccoli-Stuffed Baked Potatoes

5 (8- to 9-ounce) russet potatoes
2 tablespoons vegetable oil
2 tablespoons unsalted butter
6 cups broccoli florets, cut into 1/2- to
    1-inch pieces (discard stems)
1/2 teaspoon salt
2 tablespoons water
1 teaspoon lemon juice
1 cup (4 ounces) shredded sharp
    Cheddar cheese

1/2 cup sour cream
3 or 4 scallions, thinly sliced
    (about 1/2 cup)
1/4 cup half-and-half
2 tablespoons unsalted butter, melted
3/4 teaspoon salt
1/4 teaspoon dry mustard
Pepper to taste
1 cup (4 ounces) shredded sharp
    Cheddar cheese

Coat the potatoes with the oil and arrange on a foil-lined baking sheet. Place the baking sheet on the middle oven rack and bake at 400 degrees for 60 to 70 minutes or until a skewer inserted into the potatoes can be removed with little resistance. Cool on the baking sheet for 10 minutes.

Melt 2 tablespoons butter in a 12-inch skillet over medium-high heat. Add the broccoli and 1/2 teaspoon salt and cook for 2 minutes or until the broccoli is light brown, stirring occasionally. Add the water and cook, covered, for 1 minute or until the broccoli is tender-crisp. Remove the cover and cook for 1 minute longer or until the water evaporates. Remove the broccoli to a bowl and stir in the lemon juice.

Cut each potato lengthwise into halves. Remove the pulp using a soup spoon or melon baller, leaving about a 3/8-inch shell. Arrange the shells cut side up on a baking sheet and bake for 10 minutes or until slightly crisp. Mash the potato pulp with a fork in a bowl until smooth. Stir in 1 cup cheese, the sour cream, scallions, half-and-half, 2 tablespoons melted butter, 3/4 teaspoon salt, the dry mustard and pepper. Fold in the broccoli. Mound evenly in the shells. Sprinkle evenly with 1 cup cheese and broil for 6 to 10 minutes or until light brown. Cool for 5 minutes before serving.

Yield: 10 servings

 Nutrients Per Serving: Cal 287; Cal from Fat 165; T Fat 18.3 g; Saturated Fat 9.9 g; 57.5% Cal from Fat; Chol 43 mg; Sod 465 mg; T Carbo 20.7 g; 28.9% Cal from Carbo; Fiber 3.2 g; Prot 9.8 g; 13.7% Cal from Prot

Little Bit of Ranch Potatoes

3 potatoes, peeled and cut into
   bite-size pieces
2 to 3 tablespoons ranch
   salad dressing
2 teaspoons grated Parmesan cheese

2 tablespoons bacon bits
2 tablespoons water
1 to 2 tablespoons chopped chives
Salt and pepper to taste

Arrange the potatoes in a microwave-safe baking dish and drizzle with the salad dressing. Sprinkle with the remaining ingredients. Microwave on High for 2 to 3 minutes to soften the potatoes. Bake at 400 degrees for 30 minutes. Broil, if desired, to brown the top.

Yield: 6 servings

Nutrients Per Serving: Cal 122; Cal from Fat 40; T Fat 4.4 g; Saturated Fat 0.9 g; 32.8% Cal from Fat; Chol 5 mg; Sod 151 mg; T Carbo 17 g; 55.7% Cal from Carbo; Fiber 1.5 g; Prot 3.5 g; 11.5% Cal from Prot

Jazzy Scalloped Potatoes

5 or 6 potatoes, sliced
1 (10-ounce) can cream of celery,
   cream of chicken or cream of
   mushroom soup
1 (4-ounce) jar sliced mushrooms
1/2 cup chopped celery
1 cup frozen peas

1/4 cup milk
1 teaspoon celery salt
1/2 teaspoon pepper
1/8 teaspoon marjoram
1/8 teaspoon thyme
1 cup French-fried onions

Arrange the potatoes in a greased baking dish. Mix the soup, undrained mushrooms and celery in a saucepan and cook until heated through. Stir in the peas and milk. Spread the soup mixture evenly over the potatoes and sprinkle with the celery salt, pepper, marjoram and thyme. Toss to coat. Bake at 375 degrees until the potatoes are tender. Sprinkle with the onions and broil until brown.

Yield: 6 servings

Nutrients Per Serving: Cal 264; Cal from Fat 64; T Fat 7.1 g; Saturated Fat 2.6 g; 24.3% Cal from Fat; Chol 6 mg; Sod 548 mg; T Carbo 44 g; 66.8% Cal from Carbo; Fiber 4.6 g; Prot 5.9 g; 9% Cal from Prot

Easy Italian Spinach

2 tablespoons olive oil
2 (10-ounce) packages frozen
    chopped spinach,
    thawed and drained
1 garlic clove, chopped

1/2 cup Italian-seasoned bread crumbs
1/2 cup (2 ounces) grated Romano
    cheese
1/2 teaspoon salt
1/2 teaspoon pepper

Heat the olive oil in a nonstick skillet over medium-high heat and add the spinach and garlic. Sauté for 10 to 12 minutes or until the spinach is heated through and the liquid evaporates. Stir in the bread crumbs, cheese, salt and pepper. Serve immediately.

Yield: 6 servings

Nutrients Per Serving: Cal 138; Cal from Fat 66; T Fat 7.6 g; Saturated Fat 2.3 g; 47.7% Cal from Fat; Chol 10 mg; Sod 637 mg; T Carbo 11.4 g; 32.9% Cal from Carbo; Fiber 2.6 g; Prot 6.7 g; 19.4% Cal from Prot

Spinach Casserole

2 (10-ounce) packages frozen
    chopped spinach or broccoli
1 1/2 cups (6 ounces) shredded
    Cheddar cheese
1 (10-ounce) can cream of
    mushroom soup

1 cup mayonnaise
2 eggs, beaten
1/4 cup chopped onion
2 tablespoons margarine
1/2 cup crushed butter crackers
1/4 cup (1/2 stick) margarine, melted

Cook the spinach using the package directions and drain well. Combine the spinach, cheese, soup, mayonnaise, eggs and onion in a bowl and mix well. Spoon into a greased baking dish and dot with 2 tablespoons margarine.

Mix the cracker crumbs and 1/4 cup margarine in a bowl until coated. Sprinkle over the prepared layer and bake at 350 degrees for 35 minutes.

Yield: 6 servings

Nutrients Per Serving: Cal 481; Cal from Fat 305; T Fat 33.8 g; Saturated Fat 18.8 g; 63.4% Cal from Fat; Chol 296 mg; Sod 800 mg; T Carbo 22.4 g; 18.6% Cal from Carbo; Fiber 2.4 g; Prot 21.6 g; 18% Cal from Prot

Squash Rice Casserole

8 cups sliced zucchini (about 2¹/₂ pounds)
1 cup chopped onion
¹/₂ cup fat-free less-sodium chicken broth
2 cups cooked rice
1 cup fat-free sour cream
1 cup (4 ounces) shredded reduced-fat sharp
*   Cheddar cheese*
¹/₄ cup Italian-seasoned bread crumbs
2 eggs, lightly beaten
2 tablespoons grated fresh Parmesan cheese
1 teaspoon salt
¹/₄ teaspoon pepper
2 tablespoons grated Parmesan cheese

Combine the zucchini, onion and broth in a Dutch oven and bring to a boil. Reduce the heat to low and simmer, covered, for 20 minutes or until the zucchini is tender. Drain and partially mash the zucchini mixture. Gently stir in the rice, sour cream, Cheddar cheese, bread crumbs, eggs, 2 tablespoons Parmesan cheese, the salt and pepper.

Spoon into a 9x13-inch baking dish coated with nonstick cooking spray and sprinkle with 2 tablespoons Parmesan cheese. Bake at 350 degrees for 30 minutes or until golden brown and bubbly.

Yield: 16 servings

Nutrients Per Serving: Cal 89; Cal from Fat 17; T Fat 1.8 g; Saturated Fat 0.8 g; 19% Cal from Fat; Chol 30 mg; Sod 314 mg; T Carbo 12.5 g; 55.9% Cal from Carbo; Fiber 1.3 g; Prot 5.6 g; 25.1% Cal from Prot

Sweet Potato Casserole

Streusel

1/2 cup all-purpose flour
1/2 cup packed dark brown sugar
1/4 teaspoon salt
5 tablespoons unsalted butter,
    cut into 5 pieces and softened
1 cup pecans

Sweet Potatoes

6 (16-ounce) sweet potatoes

5 tablespoons unsalted butter, melted
4 teaspoons lemon juice
1 tablespoon vanilla extract
2 teaspoons salt
1/2 teaspoon nutmeg
1/2 teaspoon pepper
1/4 cup granulated sugar, or to taste
4 egg yolks
1 1/2 cups half-and-half

To prepare the streusel, combine the flour, brown sugar and salt in a food processor and pulse four 1-second pulses or until blended. Sprinkle 5 tablespoons butter over the top and pulse six to eight 1-second pulses or until of a crumb consistency. Sprinkle the pecans over the top and pulse five to six 1-second pulses or until combined.

To prepare the sweet potatoes, pierce the sweet potatoes several times with a sharp knife and arrange on a baking sheet lined with foil. Bake at 400 degrees for 1 to 1 1/2 hours or until the potatoes are easily squeezed easily with tongs, turning once. Cut the sweet potatoes lengthwise into halves to allow the steam to escape. Cool for 10 minutes or longer. Reduce the oven temperature to 375 degrees.

Scoop the sweet potato pulp into a large bowl. Spoon half the pulp into a food processor. Break the remaining sweet potato pulp into 1-inch chunks using a rubber spatula. Add the butter, lemon juice, vanilla, salt, nutmeg and pepper to the food processor and process for 20 seconds or until smooth. Taste for sweetness and add the granulated sugar as desired. Add the egg yolks. Add the half-and-half and process for 20 seconds or until blended. Combine the processed pulp mixture with the sweet potato pieces and mix gently until combined. Spoon into a baking dish coated with butter and spread evenly with a spatula. Sprinkle with the streusel, breaking up any large pieces. Bake for 40 to 45 minutes or until slightly puffy around the edges and brown on top. Cool for 10 minutes before serving.

Yield: 12 servings

 Nutrients Per Serving: Cal 338; Cal from Fat 191; T Fat 21.3 g; Saturated Fat 9.4 g; 56.5% Cal from Fat; Chol 107 mg; Sod 483 mg; T Carbo 32.5 g; 38.5% Cal from Carbo; Fiber 2.7 g; Prot 4.2 g; 5% Cal from Prot. *Nutritional profile includes the entire amount of the granulated sugar.*

Grilled Zucchini

8 zucchini (about 2^1/$_2$ pounds)
^{1}/$_2$ cup (1 stick) butter
2 tablespoons fresh lemon juice
1 teaspoon lemon pepper
1 teaspoon garlic powder
1 teaspoon dried oregano
^{1}/$_4$ teaspoon curry powder
Salt and pepper to taste
^{1}/$_4$ cup (1 ounce) grated Parmesan cheese

Cut the zucchini lengthwise into halves. Diagonally score the cut sides of the zucchini at 1-inch intervals, approximately ^{1}/$_4$ inch deep. Melt the butter in a heavy saucepan and stir in the lemon juice, lemon pepper, garlic powder, oregano, curry powder, salt and pepper.

Brush the butter mixture on the cut sides of the zucchini. Grill over medium heat for 10 to 12 minutes or until the zucchini is charred on all sides and slightly softened. Sprinkle the cheese over the cut sides of the zucchini. Grill, with the lid closed, for 1 minute or until the cheese begins to melt.

Yield: 8 servings

Nutrients Per Serving: Cal 134; Cal from Fat 107; T Fat 11.8 g; Saturated Fat 7.2 g; 80% Cal from Fat; Chol 31 mg; Sod 125 mg; T Carbo 4.8 g; 14.3% Cal from Carbo; Fiber 1.8 g; Prot 1.9 g; 5.7% Cal from Prot

Italian Zucchini Crescent Pie

1/4 cup (1/2 stick) butter
4 cups thinly sliced zucchini
1 cup chopped onion
2 cups (8 ounces) shredded mozzarella cheese
2 eggs, beaten
1/2 cup chopped parsley
1/2 teaspoon salt
1/2 teaspoon pepper
1/4 teaspoon garlic powder
1/4 teaspoon basil
1/4 teaspoon oregano
1 (8-count) can crescent rolls
2 tablespoons mustard

Melt the butter in a skillet and stir in the zucchini and onion. Sauté for 10 minutes and then stir in the cheese, eggs, parsley, salt, pepper, garlic powder, basil and oregano.

Unroll the crescent roll dough and separate into triangles. Press the triangles over the bottom and up the side of an ungreased 10-inch pie plate, pressing the edges to seal. Spread the mustard over the dough. Spoon the vegetable mixture into the prepared pie plate and bake at 375 degrees for 20 to 25 minutes or until cooked through. Let stand for 10 minutes before serving.

Yield: 8 servings

 Nutrients Per Serving: Cal 306; Cal from Fat 196; T Fat 21.7 g; Saturated Fat 9.3 g; 64.1% Cal from Fat; Chol 85 mg; Sod 579 mg; T Carbo 15.9 g; 20.8% Cal from Carbo; Fiber 1.2 g; Prot 11.5 g; 15.1% Cal from Prot

Cheesy Flatbread with Zucchini and Red Onion

1 (10-ounce) can refrigerator pizza dough
3/4 cup garlic and herb cheese spread, such as
    Boursin or Alouette
3/4 cup (3 ounces) finely grated Parmesan cheese
2 tablespoons chopped fresh Italian parsley
1 (8-inch) long zucchini or yellow squash,
    cut horizontally into 1/8-inch-thick rounds
1 small red onion, cut into 1/8-inch-thick rounds
Olive oil to taste
Salt and pepper to taste
1 tablespoon chopped fresh Italian parsley

Line a baking sheet with baking parchment paper and spray with nonstick cooking spray. Unroll the pizza dough on the prepared baking sheet. Spread half the herb cheese over the long side of half of the dough, leaving a 1/2-inch border. Sprinkle with half the Parmesan cheese and 2 tablespoons parsley. Using the baking parchment as an aide, fold the plain half of the dough over the cheese-topped half. Spread the remaining herb cheese over the top of the dough and sprinkle with the remaining Parmesan cheese.

Overlap the zucchini rounds in a row down the long side of the dough. Arrange overlapping onion rounds in a row alongside the zucchini. Arrange one more row of overlapping zucchini rounds alongside the onion rounds. Brush the vegetables with olive oil and sprinkle with salt and pepper. Bake at 400 degrees for 20 to 25 minutes or until puffed and dark brown around the edges. Sprinkle with 1 tablespoon parsley and cut into six slices.

Yield: 6 servings

Nutrients Per Serving: Cal 242; Cal from Fat 96; T Fat 10.9 g; Saturated Fat 6 g; 39.7% Cal from Fat; Chol 26 mg; Sod 689 mg; T Carbo 24.6 g; 40.7% Cal from Carbo; Fiber 0.8 g; Prot 11.9 g; 19.7% Cal from Prot

Four-Cheese Roasted Vegetables

2 russet potatoes, peeled and cut into
    1-inch pieces
2 carrots, cut into 1/2-inch slices
1 tablespoon olive oil
1 teaspoon basil
1 teaspoon oregano
1/4 teaspoon salt
1/4 teaspoon pepper
1 large zucchini, cut into 1/2-inch pieces
1 large red bell pepper, cut into 1-inch pieces
2 garlic cloves, minced
2 cups (8 ounces) four-cheese blend
Sprigs of basil for garnish

Arrange the potatoes and carrots in a greased 9×13-inch baking pan. Drizzle with the olive oil and sprinkle with the basil, oregano, salt and pepper. Toss lightly to coat.

Bake at 425 degrees for 20 minutes. Add the zucchini, bell pepper and garlic to the potato mixture and toss gently to combine. Bake for 20 minutes or until the vegetables are tender. Sprinkle with the cheese and bake for 2 minutes longer or until the cheese melts. Garnish with sprigs of basil.

Yield: 6 servings

Nutrients Per Serving: Cal 244; Cal from Fat 116; T Fat 13 g; Saturated Fat 7 g; 47.6% Cal from Fat; Chol 33 mg; Sod 367 mg; T Carbo 20.9 g; 34.3% Cal from Carbo; Fiber 3.8 g; Prot 11 g; 18.1% Cal from Prot

Easy Macaroni and Cheese

3 tablespoon margarine
2 1/2 cups uncooked macaroni
1/2 teaspoon salt
1/4 teaspoon pepper

8 ounces mild Cheddar
  cheese, shredded
3 to 4 cups milk

Melt the margarine in a 2-quart baking dish. Add the macaroni and stir until coated. Add the salt and pepper and mix well. Stir in the cheese. Add the milk until of the desired consistency and mix well. Bake at 325 degrees for 1 1/4 hours or until the pasta is tender.

Yield: 6 servings

Nutrients Per Serving: Cal 445; Cal from Fat 198; T Fat 22 g; Saturated Fat 11 g; 44.5% Cal from Fat; Chol 52 mg; Sod 582 mg; T Carbo 41.2 g; 37.1% Cal from Carbo; Fiber 1 g; Prot 20.5 g; 18.4% Cal from Prot

Lemon-Pecan Brown Rice

3 cups fat-free chicken broth
2 1/4 teaspoons grated lemon zest
1 tablespoon fresh lemon juice
1 tablespoon butter
1 cup brown rice

1/2 cup chopped pecans, toasted
1/4 cup chopped fresh parsley
3 tablespoons chopped green onions
2 1/4 teaspoons grated lemon zest

Bring the broth, 2 1/4 teaspoons lemon zest, the lemon juice and butter to a boil in a medium saucepan. Stir in the rice and reduce the heat to low.

Simmer, covered, for 50 to 60 minutes or until the liquid is absorbed and the rice is tender. Stir in the pecans, parsley, green onions and 2 1/4 teaspoons lemon zest. Serve immediately.

Yield: 4 servings

Nutrients Per Serving: Cal 304; Cal from Fat 125; T Fat 14 g; Saturated Fat 2.9 g; 41.1% Cal from Fat; Chol 8 mg; Sod 372 mg; T Carbo 39.3 g; 51.7% Cal from Carbo; Fiber 2.8 g; Prot 5.4 g; 7.1% Cal from Prot

Rice Pilaf with Pecans and Dried Cranberries

3/4 cup pecans
8 sprigs of thyme
13/4 cups canned low-sodium
    chicken broth
1/4 cup water
2 bay leaves
1 cup wild rice, sorted and rinsed
11/2 cups long grain white rice
3 tablespoons unsalted butter

11/4 cups finely chopped onions
1 cup finely chopped carrots
1 teaspoon salt
21/4 cups water
3/4 cup sweetened or unsweetened
    dried cranberries
11/2 tablespoons minced fresh
    Italian parsley
Salt and pepper to taste

Toast the pecans in an ungreased small skillet over medium heat for 6 minutes or until fragrant and light brown. Remove the pecans to a plate to cool and coarsely chop. Divide the thyme sprigs into two bundles and tie each bundle with kitchen twine.

Bring one thyme bundle, the broth, 1/4 cup water and the bay leaves to a boil in a medium saucepan over medium-high heat. Stir in the wild rice. Reduce the heat to low and simmer, covered, for 35 to 45 minutes or until the rice is plump and tender and most of the liquid has been absorbed. Drain the rice in a mesh strainer and discard the bay leaves and thyme bundle. Return the rice to the saucepan and cover to keep warm.

Place the white rice in a bowl and add enough water to cover by two inches. Gently swirl the bowl to release any excess starch; drain. Repeat this process about five times or until the water almost runs clear. Drain the rice in a mesh strainer. Heat the butter in a medium saucepan over medium-high heat for 2 minutes or until the foam subsides. Stir in the onions, carrots and 1 teaspoon salt. Cook for 4 minutes or until the vegetables are tender but not brown. Add the white rice and stir until the grains are coated with the butter. Cook for 3 minutes or just until the grains begin to turn translucent, stirring frequently.

Bring 21/4 cups water to a boil in a small saucepan or microwave-safe bowl. Add the boiling water and remaining thyme bundle to the white rice mixture and return to a boil. Reduce the heat to low and sprinkle the cranberries over the top. Simmer, covered, for 16 to 18 minutes or until all of the liquid is absorbed. Remove from the heat and discard the thyme bundle. Fluff the rice with a fork. Combine the wild rice, white rice mixture, pecans and parsley in a bowl and mix well. Taste and adjust the seasonings with salt and pepper to taste. Serve immediately.

Yield: 8 servings

Nutrients Per Serving: Cal 371; Cal from Fat 109; T Fat 12 g; Saturated Fat 3.4 g; 29.4% Cal from Fat; Chol 12 mg; Sod 431 mg; T Carbo 58.1 g; 62.6% Cal from Carbo; Fiber 4.2 g; Prot 7.4 g; 8% Cal from Prot

Meats & Poultry

GERD

Food enters the body through the mouth, traveling down the esophagus and into the stomach. At the junction of the esophagus and the stomach, there is a muscular structure known as the lower esophageal sphincter. This sphincter normally stays open for 5 to 10 seconds to allow food to enter the stomach. Gastroesophageal reflux disease (**GERD**) develops when the valve fails to close properly and food and gastric acid reenter the esophagus. Symptoms of this disorder may include heartburn, acid regurgitation, and difficulty swallowing.

GERD may result in conditions known as nonerosive reflux disease, erosive esophagitis, or Barrett's esophagus. After one of these conditions is diagnosed, the administration of medications to decrease stomach acid plays a key role. The treatment and its success also involves lifestyle changes.

Some of the changes may include:

- Avoiding trigger foods, such as hot and spicy foods, citrus, caffeine, chocolate, alcohol, carbonated beverages, and cigarettes.
- Eating three balanced meals a day and reducing your portion size.
- Not eating for two to three hours prior to bedtime.
- Shedding extra weight, which helps decrease pressure on your abdomen.
- Avoiding tight clothing and tight belts.
- **Strict adherence to your physician's orders and prescribed medications.**

Holiday Beef Tenderloin with Spiced Cranberry Pear Chutney

Tenderloin

1 to 2 tablespoons cracked
  pepper
3 garlic cloves, minced
2 teaspoons dried thyme leaves
1 (4-pound) whole beef
  tenderloin, trimmed
Salt to taste

Spiced Cranberry Pear Chutney

3 large ripe pears, cut into
  1/2-inch pieces
1 small onion, chopped
1/2 cup sweetened dried cranberries
1/2 cup packed brown sugar
1/4 cup cider vinegar
1 jalapeño chile, seeded and
  finely chopped
1 tablespoon fresh lime juice
1/4 teaspoon ground allspice

To prepare the tenderloin, mix the pepper, garlic and thyme in a small bowl. Rub over the surface of the tenderloin. Arrange the tenderloin on a rack in a shallow roasting pan and insert an ovenproof meat thermometer in the thickest portion of the tenderloin; do not allow to rest on fat.

Roast at 425 degrees for 50 to 60 minutes or until the meat thermometer registers 135 degrees for medium-rare, or 60 to 70 minutes or until the meat thermometer registers 150 degrees for medium. Remove to a carving board and tent loosely with foil. Let stand for 15 to 20 minutes. The temperature will continue to rise about 10 degrees to reach 145 degrees for medium-rare and 160 degrees for medium. Cut into thick slices and season with salt.

To prepare the chutney, combine the pears, onion, cranberries, brown sugar, vinegar, jalapeño chile, lime juice and allspice in a saucepan and bring to a boil. Reduce the heat to low and simmer for 30 minutes or until thickened, stirring occasionally. Serve warm or at room temperature with the tenderloin.

Note: The chutney may be prepared up to 2 days in advance and stored, covered, in the refrigerator. Reheat or bring to room temperature before serving.

Yield: 8 servings

 Nutrients Per Serving: Cal 526; Cal from Fat 186; T Fat 20.6 g; Saturated Fat 8 g; 35.3% Cal from Fat; Chol 144 mg; Sod 128 mg; T Carbo 37.3 g; 28.3% Cal from Carbo; Fiber 3.3 g; Prot 47.8 g; 36.3% Cal from Prot. *Nutritional profile includes all of the chutney.*

Beef Stroganoff

2 pounds sirloin steak, cut into thin strips
2 cups sliced fresh mushrooms
2 onions, sliced
2 tablespoons vegetable oil
1/2 cup hot water
1/2 cup red wine
2 beef bouillon cubes
2 tablespoons ketchup
1 teaspoon dry mustard
1/2 teaspoon salt
2 tablespoons all-purpose flour
1/2 cup water
1 cup sour cream
12 ounces noodles, cooked

Brown the steak with the mushrooms and onions in the oil in a large skillet; drain. Stir in 1/2 cup hot water, the wine, bouillon cubes, ketchup, dry mustard and salt. Simmer, covered, for 30 minutes or until the steak is tender, stirring occasionally.

Whisk the flour and 1/2 cup water in a bowl until blended and stir into the steak mixture. Increase the heat and bring to a boil, stirring constantly. At this point the mixture may be stored in the refrigerator for up to 1 day. Reduce the heat and stir in the sour cream. Cook just until heated through; do not boil. Spoon over the hot noodles on a platter.

Yield: 6 servings

Nutrients Per Serving: Cal 702; Cal from Fat 332; T Fat 36.7 g; Saturated Fat 14.7 g; 47.3% Cal from Fat; Chol 118 mg; Sod 669 mg; T Carbo 53.4 g; 30.4% Cal from Carbo; Fiber 3.6 g; Prot 39 g; 22.2% Cal from Prot

Sliced Roast Beef in Mushroom Sauce

3/4 cup sliced onion
2 tablespoons butter
4 ounces mushrooms, sliced
3/4 cup beef broth
1/3 cup dry red wine
1/4 cup ketchup

2 tablespoons all-purpose flour
1 teaspoon salt
1/4 teaspoon freshly ground pepper
1/4 teaspoon marjoram
8 (2-ounce) slices cooked roast beef

Sauté the onion in the butter in a large skillet for 5 minutes. Stir in the mushrooms and sauté for 5 minutes longer. Whisk the broth, wine and ketchup in a bowl until blended. Add the flour, salt, pepper and marjoram and whisk until smooth.

Add to the mushroom mixture and mix well. Simmer for 10 minutes, stirring constantly. Pour the mushroom sauce over the roast beef in a skillet and simmer just until heated through.

Yield: 4 servings

Nutrients Per Serving: Cal 513; Cal from Fat 338; T Fat 37.6 g; Saturated Fat 16.2 g; 65.9% Cal from Fat; Chol 133 mg; Sod 1049 mg; T Carbo 11.9 g; 9.3% Cal from Carbo; Fiber 1.1 g; Prot 31.8 g; 24.8% Cal from Prot

ACCORDING TO THE USDA, ALL ALCOHOL DOES NOT EVAPORATE IN COOKING. AFTER 15 MINUTES OF COOKING, 40 PERCENT OF THE ALOCHOL REMAINS; AFTER 90 MINUTES, 20 PERCENT OF THE ALCOHOL REMAINS.

Miniature Meat Loaves

3/4 cup milk
1 egg, beaten
1 cup (4 ounces) shredded Cheddar cheese
1/2 cup bread crumbs
1/2 cup chopped onion
1 teaspoon salt
1 pound ground beef
2/3 cup ketchup
1/2 cup packed brown sugar
1/2 cup mustard

Combine the milk, egg, cheese, bread crumbs, onion and salt in a bowl and mix well. Add the ground beef and mix well. Shape into six individual loaves and arrange in a greased baking dish.

Mix the ketchup, brown sugar and mustard in a bowl and spoon over the loaves. Bake at 350 degrees for 45 minutes; drain.

Yield: 6 servings

Nutrients Per Serving: Cal 654; Cal from Fat 428; T Fat 47.6 g; Saturated Fat 15.6 g; 65.4% Cal from Fat; Chol 124 mg; Sod 1006 mg; T Carbo 34.8 g; 21.3% Cal from Carbo; Fiber 0.5 g; Prot 21.7 g; 13.3% Cal from Prot

Chili Mac

8 cups prepared macaroni and cheese
2 pounds ground beef
1 envelope chili seasoning mix
1 (6-ounce) can chopped green chiles
1 (8-ounce) can corn
Chopped red and green bell peppers to taste
1 (15-ounce) can chili-style tomatoes or diced tomatoes
Salt and pepper to taste
2 cups (8 ounces) shredded Mexican taco cheese
Sour cream for garnish

Grease a 9×13-inch baking pan or spray with nonstick cooking spray. Spread the macaroni and cheese in the prepared pan. Brown the ground beef in a skillet, stirring until crumbly; drain. Stir in the chili seasoning, green chiles, corn, bell peppers and tomatoes and cook using the package directions for the chili seasoning. Season with salt and pepper.

Spoon the ground beef mixture over the prepared layer and sprinkle with the cheese. Bake at 350 degrees for 20 minutes or until brown and bubbly. Let stand for 15 minutes before serving. Garnish each serving with a dollop of sour cream.

Yield: 8 servings

 Nutrients Per Serving: Cal 849; Cal from Fat 473; T Fat 52.4 g; Saturated Fat 25.2 g; Chol 165 mg; Sod 1573 mg; T Carbo 53.3 g; Fiber 5.5 g; Prot 40.8 g

Lasagna

16 ounces lasagna noodles
1 pound ground beef
1 pound smoked beef sausage, casings removed
1 (32-ounce) jar garden-style Ragú sauce
1 (16-ounce) jar Ragú sauce with mushrooms
16 ounces cottage cheese or ricotta cheese
12 ounces mozzarella cheese, shredded
3/4 cup (3 ounces) grated Parmesan cheese

Cook the noodles using the package directions; drain. Brown the ground beef and sausage in a skillet, stirring until crumbly; drain. Stir in the sauces and simmer to the desired consistency, stirring occasionally. Mix the cottage cheese and mozzarella cheese in a bowl.

Layer one-third of the of the meat sauce, half the noodles, half the remaining meat sauce, half the cottage cheese mixture, the remaining noodles, the remaining meat sauce and the remaining cottage cheese mixture in a greased 9×13-inch baking dish. Sprinkle with the Parmesan cheese and bake at 375 degrees for 30 minutes.

Yield: 8 servings

Nutrients Per Serving: Cal 969; Cal from Fat 495; T Fat 55.1 g; Saturated Fat 23.1 g; 51.1% Cal from Fat; Chol 140 mg; Sod 1841 mg; T Carbo 72.3 g; 29.9% Cal from Carbo; Fiber 7.3 g; Prot 46.1 g; 19% Cal from Prot

Sunday-Night Lasagna

1 pound ground beef
1/2 cup chopped onion
2 (25-ounce) jars pasta sauce
1 (14-ounce) can diced tomatoes
3 (6-ounce) cans tomato paste
16 ounces ricotta cheese
8 ounces mozzarella cheese, shredded
1 cup (4 ounces) grated Parmesan cheese
2 eggs, lightly beaten
8 ounces lasagna noodles
1/4 cup (1 ounce) grated Parmesan cheese

Brown the ground beef with the onion in a skillet, stirring until the ground beef is crumbly; drain. Stir in the pasta sauce, tomatoes and tomato paste and simmer for 30 minutes, stirring occasionally. Mix the ricotta cheese, mozzarella cheese, 1 cup Parmesan cheese and the eggs in a bowl.

Layer the meat sauce, uncooked noodles and ricotta cheese mixture in a 9×13-inch baking dish until all of the ingredients are used, beginning and ending with the meat sauce. Sprinkle with 1/4 cup Parmesan cheese. Bake, covered with foil, at 350 degrees for 45 minutes. Remove the foil and bake for 15 minutes longer.

Yield: 8 servings

Nutrients Per Serving: Cal 827; Cal from Fat 391; T Fat 43.7 g; Saturated Fat 20.2 g; 47.3% Cal from Fat; Chol 168 mg; Sod 1824 mg; T Carbo 69.4 g; 33.6% Cal from Carbo; Fiber 10 g; Prot 39.6 g; 19.2% Cal from Prot

Spaghetti and Meatballs

1 pound ground beef
1/2 cup seasoned bread crumbs
1/2 cup (2 ounces) grated Parmesan cheese
1/3 cup chopped onion
1/4 cup milk
2 eggs, lightly beaten
2 garlic cloves, minced
1/2 teaspoon pepper
8 cups spaghetti sauce
16 ounces spaghetti

Combine the ground beef, bread crumbs, cheese, onion, milk, eggs, garlic and pepper in a bowl and mix well. Shape into 1-inch meatballs.

Bring the sauce to a boil in a 5-quart Dutch oven and carefully add the meatballs. Return to a boil and then reduce the heat to low. Simmer, partially covered, for 25 minutes or until the meatballs are cooked through.

Cook the spaghetti using the package directions; drain. Toss the hot spaghetti with 1 cup of the sauce in a pasta bowl. Spoon the remaining sauce and meatballs over the pasta mixture. Serve immediately.

Note: For a healthier entrée, use ground turkey and whole wheat spaghetti.

Yield: 8 servings

Nutrients Per Serving: Cal 1558; Cal from Fat 538; T Fat 59.8 g; Saturated Fat 17 g; 34.5% Cal from Fat; Chol 107 mg; Sod 4833 mg; T Carbo 215.1 g; 55.2% Cal from Carbo; Fiber 33.8 g; Prot 39.8 g; 10.2% Cal from Prot

Swedish Meatballs

2 pounds ground beef
12 saltine crackers, crushed
1 small onion, chopped
1/4 cup ketchup
2 eggs, lightly beaten
1 tablespoon prepared mustard
1 tablespoon parsley flakes
1 (12-ounce) jar chili sauce
1 (32-ounce) jar grape jelly

Combine the ground beef, cracker crumbs, onion, ketchup, eggs, mustard and parsley flakes in a bowl and mix well. Shape into 2-inch meatballs. Brown the meatballs in a skillet; drain.

Place the meatballs in a slow cooker and pour the chili sauce over the top. Stir in the grape jelly. Cook for 1 hour or until the jelly melts and blends with the chili sauce, stirring occasionally. Serve with mashed potatoes, pasta or rice.

Yield: 10 servings

Nutrients Per Serving: Cal 600; Cal from Fat 240; T Fat 26.8 g; Saturated Fat 10.3 g; 40% Cal from Fat; Chol 119 mg; Sod 1121 mg; T Carbo 73.2 g; 48.8% Cal from Carbo; Fiber 0.2 g; Prot 16.7 g; 11.1% Cal from Prot

Reuben Loaf

1 envelope dry yeast
1 cup warm water (105 to 115 degrees)
1 tablespoon margarine
1 tablespoon sugar
1 teaspoon salt
3¹/4 cups all-purpose flour
¹/4 cup Thousand Island salad dressing
8 ounces corned beef, thinly sliced
4 ounces Swiss cheese, thinly sliced
1 (27-ounce) can sauerkraut, drained
1 egg white, beaten
¹/2 teaspoon caraway seeds

Combine the yeast, warm water, margarine, sugar and salt in a large bowl and mix well. Reserve 1 cup of the flour. Mix in just enough of the remaining flour to make a soft dough, adding the reserved flour as needed.

Roll the dough into a rectangle on a lightly greased baking sheet. Score the rectangle lengthwise into three equal sections. Spread the salad dressing over the center section. Layer the corned beef, cheese and sauerkraut one-half at a time over the salad dressing. Cross the sides over the center to enclose the filling and form a loaf, sealing the edges. Brush with the egg white and sprinkle with the caraway seeds. Bake at 350 degrees for 30 minutes. Slice as desired.

Yield: 6 servings

 Nutrients Per Serving: Cal 477; Cal from Fat 136; T Fat 15.2 g; Saturated Fat 5.8 g; Chol 79 mg; Sod 1899 mg; T Carbo 62.7 g; Fiber 5.3 g; Prot 22.6 g. *Nutritional profile includes all of the flour.*

Cranberry Orange Pork Roast

1 (3-pound) pork loin roast
1 teaspoon cumin seeds or
    ground cumin
1 teaspoon ginger
1 teaspoon celery salt

Pepper to taste
2 tablespoons Dijon mustard or spicy
    brown mustard
1 (14-ounce) can cranberry sauce
1 orange

Place the roast in a slow cooker and sprinkle with the cumin, ginger, celery salt and pepper. Spread the Dijon mustard over the surface of the roast and cover with the cranberry sauce. Cut the orange into 1/4- to 1/8-inch slices and arrange around the roast. Cook on High for 5 to 6 hours or on Low for 10 to 12 hours or until the roast is cooked through.

Yield: 6 servings

Nutrients Per Serving: Cal 608; Cal from Fat 302; T Fat 33.5 g; Saturated Fat 10.5 g; Chol 152 mg; Sod 160 mg; T Carbo 30.4 g; Fiber 1.6 g; Prot 46.2 g

Pork Chops with Green Apples

4 (5-ounce) pork chops
1/2 cup olive oil
2 or 3 Granny Smith apples, peeled
    and sliced
4 garlic cloves, pressed

3/4 to 1 cup chopped white or
    yellow onion
1 teaspoon cornstarch
1 tablespoon water

Fry the pork chops in the olive oil in a nonstick skillet until light brown, turning frequently. Stir in the apples, garlic and onion.

Cook, covered, over medium heat for 1 hour or until the pork chops are cooked through. Dissolve the cornstarch in the water in a bowl and add to the pork chop mixture. Cook just until slightly thickened. Serve with mashed potatoes or jasmine white rice.

Yield: 4 servings

Nutrients Per Serving: Cal 722; Cal from Fat 440; T Fat 49 g; Saturated Fat 12 g; 60.9% Cal from Fat; Chol 103 mg; Sod 58 mg; T Carbo 32 g; 17.7% Cal from Carbo; Fiber 3.4 g; Prot 38.6 g; 21.4% Cal from Prot

Jambalaya

8 ounces chaurice, chorizo or spicy
   smoked sausage, casings removed
2 tablespoons unsalted butter
1 large onion, chopped
2 garlic cloves, minced
1 large green bell pepper, chopped
1 large red bell pepper, chopped
2 large tomatoes, seeded and chopped
1 teaspoon chopped fresh thyme, or
   1/2 teaspoon dried thyme

1 teaspoon chili powder
1/4 teaspoon cayenne pepper
1/16 teaspoon sugar
1 cup long grain rice
1 cup chopped smoked ham
1 1/2 cups chicken stock
1 pound small shrimp, peeled and
   deveined
3 tablespoons chopped fresh parsley

Sauté the sausage in a greased heavy saucepan or Dutch oven over medium heat until brown. Remove the sausage to a platter and discard the pan drippings. Add the butter and onion to the saucepan and cook over medium-low heat for 2 minutes, scraping the bottom and side of the saucepan to dislodge any browned bits. Stir in the garlic and cook for 3 minutes. Add the bell peppers, tomatoes, thyme, chili powder, cayenne pepper and sugar and mix well. Reduce the heat to low and cook, covered, for 15 minutes.

Slice the sausage and add to the saucepan. Stir in the rice, ham and stock and bring to a boil. Reduce the heat to low and simmer, covered, for 30 minutes or until the rice is tender. Stir in the shrimp and cook, covered, for 5 minutes or until the shrimp turn pink. Remove the cover if the jambalaya is too moist and cook over low heat until of a thicker consistency. Mix in the parsley just before serving. Ladle into bowls.

Yield: 4 servings

Nutrients Per Serving: Cal 750; Cal from Fat 300; T Fat 33.3 g; Saturated Fat 13.3 g; Chol 264 mg; Sod 2166 mg; T Carbo 56.1 g; Fiber 3.5 g; Prot 56.3 g

Beef Marinade

$^1/_2$ cup vegetable oil
$^1/_2$ cup red wine
$^1/_4$ cup soy sauce
$^1/_4$ cup Worcestershire sauce
2 tablespoons teriyaki sauce
1 tablespoon minced garlic

1 teaspoon black pepper
1 teaspoon crushed red pepper
1 teaspoon onion powder, or
   1 tablespoon onion soup mix
1 teaspoon hot red pepper sauce

Whisk the oil, wine, soy sauce, Worcestershire sauce, teriyaki sauce, garlic, black pepper, red pepper, onion powder and hot sauce in a bowl until combined. Add 1 to 2 pounds of beef of choice.

Marinate in the refrigerator for 1 to 24 hours, turning occasionally. Drain and grill to the desired degree of doneness.

Makes about 1$^3/_4$ cups

Nutrients Per Serving: *Nutritional profile is not available for this recipe.*

Ginger Ale Barbecue

1$^1/_2$ cups ginger ale
$^3/_4$ cup ketchup
$^3/_4$ tablespoon brown sugar

$^3/_4$ teaspoon prepared mustard
1 pound chipped ham

Combine the ginger ale, ketchup, brown sugar and mustard in a saucepan and mix well. Bring to a boil over medium-high heat and then reduce the heat to low. Simmer for 1 hour, stirring occasionally. Serve over the ham.

Note: Serve the sauce with beef, pork or chicken.

Yield: 4 servings

Nutrients Per Serving: Cal 320; Cal from Fat 185; T Fat 20.7 g; Saturated Fat 6.6 g; 57.8% Cal from Fat; Chol 56 mg; Sod 2089 mg; T Carbo 13.6 g; 17% Cal from Carbo; Fiber 0.6 g; Prot 20.1 g; 25.1% Cal from Prot

Chicken Spaghetti

5 pounds chicken (whole or pieces)
16 ounces spaghetti
1/2 cup chopped celery
1/2 cup chopped onion
1/2 cup (1 stick) margarine
2 (10-ounce) cans cream of mushroom soup
1 (10-ounce) can cream of celery soup
1 (10-ounce) can cream of chicken soup
1 (6-ounce) can large mushrooms
1 (8-ounce) jar Cheez Whiz
1/8 teaspoon salt
1/8 teaspoon pepper
1/8 teaspoon poultry seasoning
5 or 6 drops of Tabasco sauce

Combine the chicken with enough water to cover in a stockpot and bring to a boil. Boil for 30 to 40 minutes or until cooked through. Remove the chicken to a platter, reserving the broth. Let stand until cool. Chop the chicken into bite-size pieces, discarding the skin and bones. Cook the spaghetti in the reserved broth until al dente; drain. Cover to keep warm.

Sauté the celery and onion in the margarine in a saucepan until tender. Stir in the soups and mushrooms and cook until heated through, stirring frequently. Combine the spaghetti, chicken, soup mixture, Cheez Whiz, salt, pepper, poultry seasoning and Tabasco sauce in a large bowl and mix well. Serve immediately.

Yield: 12 servings

 Nutrients Per Serving: Cal 754; Cal from Fat 376; T Fat 41.9 g; Saturated Fat 12.2 g; 49.8% Cal from Fat; Chol 167 mg; Sod 1314 mg; T Carbo 38.6 g; 20.5% Cal from Carbo; Fiber 1.6 g; Prot 56 g; 29.7% Cal from Prot

Chili Chicken with Pineapple

Chicken

1 garlic clove, pressed
1/4 teaspoon salt
1 (3-pound) chicken, skinned,
    deboned and cut into
    bite-size pieces
1 tablespoon corn flour
2 tablespoons sesame oil
5 or 6 spring onions, sliced
2 or 3 green bell peppers, cut into
    bite-size pieces
1 rib celery, chopped
3 pineapple slices, cut into
    3/4-inch pieces

Ginger-Soy Sauce and Assembly

2 cups chicken stock
2 tablespoons ginger sherry
2 tablespoons soy sauce
1 tablespoon vinegar
1 tablespoon corn flour
1 teaspoon sesame seed oil
1/2 teaspoon sugar
Hot fried rice

To prepare the chicken, mix the garlic and salt in a small bowl until of a paste consistency. Pat the garlic paste over the chicken and chill, covered, for 3 to 4 hours. Coat the chicken with the corn flour.

Heat the sesame oil in a skillet and add the chicken pieces. Cook over low heat until the chicken is brown and cooked through. Remove to a platter using a slotted spoon, reserving the pan drippings. Add the onions to the reserved pan drippings and sauté. Stir in the bell peppers and sauté until the vegetables are tender. Remove from the heat and stir in the chicken, celery and pineapple.

To prepare the sauce, combine the stock, sherry, soy sauce, vinegar, corn flour, sesame seed oil and sugar in a bowl and mix well.

Pour the sauce mixture into a large saucepan and cook until thickened, stirring occasionally. Stir the chicken mixture into the sauce and cook just until heated through. Serve over fried rice with chili sauce.

Yield: 4 servings

 Nutrients Per Serving: Cal 587; Cal from Fat 181; T Fat 20.1 g; Saturated Fat 4.3 g; 30.8% Cal from Fat; Chol 240 mg; Sod 1785 mg; T Carbo 21.6 g; 14.7% Cal from Carbo; Fiber 3.8 g; Prot 80 g; 54.5% Cal from Prot. *Nutritional profile does not include fried rice or chili sauce.*

Chicken Tortilla Casserole

1 (3-pound) chicken
2 (3-ounce) cans green chiles, drained
2 (10-ounce) cans cream of mushroom soup
1 (10-ounce) cans cream of chicken soup
1 large onion, finely chopped
10 ounces extra-sharp Cheddar cheese, shredded
12 (6-inch) corn tortillas, cut into 1-inch pieces

Roast the chicken in a baking pan at 400 degrees for 1 hour or until the juices run clear. Let stand until cool. Cut into large chunks, discarding the skin and bones. Remove the seeds from the green chiles and cut the chiles into large strips. Combine the soups, onion and half the cheese in a bowl and mix well.

Layer the soup mixture, tortillas, chicken, green chiles and remaining cheese in a buttered 9×13-inch baking dish. Chill, covered, for 24 hours. Bake, covered, at 300 degrees for 1 1/2 hours. You may freeze, unbaked, for future use.

Yield: 8 servings

Nutrients Per Serving: Cal 695; Cal from Fat 373; T Fat 41.6 g; Saturated Fat 15.7 g; 53.7% Cal from Fat; Chol 173 mg; Sod 1238 mg; T Carbo 25.4 g; 14.6% Cal from Carbo; Fiber 2.6 g; Prot 55.1 g; 31.7% Cal from Prot

Chicken Supreme

3 cups coarsely chopped cooked chicken breasts
1 (10-ounce) can cream of chicken soup
1 soup can milk
1 (7-ounce) package chicken-flavor rice
1 (8-ounce) can water chestnuts, drained and sliced
1 cup chopped celery
1 cup chopped onion
1 cup chicken broth
3/4 cup mayonnaise
1/4 cup crushed potato chips

Combine the chicken, soup, milk, rice, water chestnuts, celery, onion, broth and mayonnaise in a bowl and mix well. Spoon into a 9×14-inch baking pan. Chill, covered, for 8 to 10 hours.

Sprinkle the chilled layer with the potato chips. Bake at 325 degrees for 1 hour. Let stand for 5 minutes before serving.

Yield: 8 servings

Nutrients Per Serving: Cal 586; Cal from Fat 196; T Fat 21.8 g; Saturated Fat 4.1 g; 33.4% Cal from Fat; Chol 59 mg; Sod 1147 mg; T Carbo 75.1 g; 51.2% Cal from Carbo; Fiber 2 g; Prot 22.5 g; 15.3% Cal from Prot

Almond Lemon Chicken

Marinade
5 tablespoons lemon juice
3 tablespoons Dijon mustard
2 garlic cloves, chopped
1/4 teaspoon white pepper
5 tablespoons olive oil

Chicken
4 (5-ounce) boneless skinless
    chicken breasts, sliced

1 tablespoon olive oil
2 cups chicken broth
1 teaspoon cornstarch
2 tablespoons lemon or
    orange marmalade
2 tablespoons butter
2 tablespoons parsley
1/4 teaspoon red pepper flakes
1 cup sliced almonds, toasted

To prepare the marinade, mix the lemon juice, Dijon mustard, garlic and white pepper in a bowl. Add the olive oil gradually, whisking constantly until the oil is incorporated.

To prepare the chicken, pour the marinade over the chicken in a shallow dish, turning to coat. Marinate, covered, in the refrigerator for 1 hour, turning occasionally. Drain, reserving the marinade.

Sauté the chicken in the olive oil in a skillet for 6 to 10 minutes or until the chicken is cooked through. Stir in the reserved marinade. Whisk the broth and cornstarch in a bowl until blended and add to the skillet. Cook for 5 minutes or until thickened, stirring frequently. Mix in the marmalade, butter, parsley and red pepper flakes and cook just until heated through. Sprinkle with the almonds and serve with green beans and hot cooked rice.

Yield: 4 servings

Nutrients Per Serving: Cal 809; Cal from Fat 558; T Fat 62 g; Saturated Fat 10.6 g; 69% Cal from Fat; Chol 100 mg; Sod 948 mg; T Carbo 16.4 g; 8.1% Cal from Carbo; Fiber 4.6 g; Prot 46.4 g; 22.9% Cal from Prot

Chicken Cordon Bleu

6 (5-ounce) boneless skinless
   chicken breasts
6 (1-ounce) slices ham
3 (1-ounce) slices mozzarella cheese,
   cut into halves

1 tomato, seeded and chopped
1/3 cup bread crumbs
2 tablespoons grated Parmesan cheese
2 tablespoons parsley
1/2 cup (1 stick) butter, melted

Pound the chicken breasts between sheets of waxed paper with a meat mallet until thin. Layer each chicken breast with one slice of the ham and one slice of the cheese. Top equally with the tomato. Roll to enclose the filling and seal all the edges with wooden picks. Mix the bread crumbs, cheese and parsley in a shallow dish. Dip the chicken rolls in the butter and then coat with the crumb mixture. Arrange the chicken rolls in a single layer in a baking dish and bake at 350 degrees for 1 hour.

Yield: 6 servings

 Nutrients Per Serving: Cal 409; Cal from Fat 210; T Fat 23.3 g; Saturated Fat 13 g; 51.3% Cal from Fat; Chol 149 mg; Sod 780 mg; T Carbo 6.7 g; 6.5% Cal from Carbo; Fiber 0.3 g; Prot 43.1 g; 42.1% Cal from Prot

Chicken with Wine Sauce

4 (5-ounce) boneless skinless
   chicken breasts
1 cup (4 ounces) shredded Swiss
   cheese
1/4 cup dry white wine

1 (10-ounce) can cream of chicken or
   cream of mushroom soup
1 (16-ounce) package herb-seasoned
   stuffing mix
1/3 cup butter, melted

Arrange the chicken in a single layer in a 9×13-inch baking dish and sprinkle with the cheese. Mix the wine and soup in a bowl and pour over the chicken. Sprinkle with the stuffing mix and drizzle with the butter. Bake at 350 degrees for 50 to 55 minutes or until the chicken is cooked through.

Yield: 4 servings

 Nutrients Per Serving: Cal 890; Cal from Fat 296; T Fat 33 g; Saturated Fat 17.3 g; 33.3% Cal from Fat; Chol 155 mg; Sod 2682 mg; T Carbo 93.1 g; 41.8% Cal from Carbo; Fiber 3.7 g; Prot 55.4 g; 24.9% Cal from Prot

Chicken Marsala

2¹/₂ ounces pancetta
1 cup all-purpose flour
4 (5-ounce) boneless skinless
   chicken breasts
Salt and pepper to taste
2 tablespoons vegetable oil
8 ounces white mushrooms, sliced
1 garlic clove, minced

1 teaspoon tomato paste
1¹/₂ cups sweet marsala
1¹/₂ tablespoons fresh lemon juice
¹/₄ cup (¹/₂ stick) unsalted butter,
   cut into tablespoons
2 tablespoons chopped fresh
   Italian parsley

Cut the pancetta into strips 1 inch long and ¹/₈ inch wide. Adjust the oven rack to the lower-middle position and place a baking dish on the oven rack. Heat the oven to 200 degrees. Heat a 12-inch heavy skillet over medium-high heat until very hot. Pour the flour into a shallow dish. Season both sides of the chicken with salt and pepper and coat one chicken breast at a time with the flour. Lift the chicken from the flour using tongs and shake to remove any excess flour.

Pour the oil into the hot skillet and heat until simmering. Arrange the chicken in a single layer in the hot oil and cook for 3 minutes or until golden brown. Turn the chicken and cook for 3 minutes longer or until golden brown and firm to the touch. Remove the chicken to the heated baking dish using a slotted spoon and return the baking dish to the oven, reserving the pan drippings. Add the pancetta to the reserved pan drippings and cook over low heat for 4 minutes or until brown and crisp, stirring occasionally and scraping the bottom of the skillet to loosen any browned bits. Remove the pancetta with a slotted spoon to a paper towel to drain, reserving the pan drippings. Add the mushrooms to the reserved pan drippings and increase the heat to medium-high.

Sauté for 8 minutes or until the liquid evaporates and the mushrooms begin to brown. Stir in the garlic, tomato paste and pancetta and sauté for 1 minute or until the tomato paste begins to brown. Remove from the heat and stir in the wine. Cook over high heat for 5 minutes or until the sauce is reduced to 1¹/₄ cups and is of a slightly syrupy consistency, stirring frequently and scraping any browned bits from the bottom of the skillet. Remove from the heat and stir in accumulated juices from the chicken and the lemon juice. Whisk in the butter 1 tablespoon at a time until combined. Season with salt and pepper and stir in the parsley. Spoon over the chicken on a platter and serve immediately.

Yield: 4 servings

Nutrients Per Serving: Cal 479; Cal from Fat 196; T Fat 21.7 g; Saturated Fat 9.9 g; 40.9% Cal from Fat; Chol 129 mg; Sod 437 mg; T Carbo 30.2 g; 25.2% Cal from Carbo; Fiber 1.7 g; Prot 40.5 g; 33.8% Cal from Prot

Chicken Manicotti Carbonara

1¹/2 pounds boneless skinless chicken breasts, sliced
    or chicken tenders
1 teaspoon garlic powder
4 cups refrigerator Alfredo sauce
1 cup skim milk
14 ounces manicotti
1 cup (4 ounces) freshly shredded Parmesan cheese
1 cup frozen small peas, thawed
¹/2 cup julienned cooked ham

Sprinkle the chicken with garlic powder. Mix the sauce and milk in a bowl. Spread 1 cup of the sauce mixture over the bottom of a 9×13-inch baking dish.

Fill the pasta evenly with the chicken; stuff into each end. Arrange the stuffed pasta in the prepared baking dish. Reserve ¹/2 cup of the remaining sauce mixture and pour the remaining sauce mixture over the pasta. Bake, covered tightly with foil, at 350 degrees for 1¹/4 hours.

Combine the reserved ¹/2 cup sauce mixture, the cheese, peas and ham in a bowl and mix well. Pour over the baked pasta. Bake, uncovered, for 15 to 20 minutes longer or until the cheese melts. Let stand for 10 minutes before serving.

Yield: 7 servings

 Nutrients Per Serving: Cal 646; Cal from Fat 254; T Fat 28.1 g; Saturated Fat 14.7 g; 39.3% Cal from Fat; Chol 188 mg; Sod 1434 mg; T Carbo 54 g; 33.4% Cal from Carbo; Fiber 3 g; Prot 44.1 g; 27.3% Cal from Prot

Chicken with Sesame Noodles

1/4 cup sesame seeds

5 tablespoons soy sauce

1/4 cup chunky peanut butter

3 tablespoons light brown sugar

2 tablespoons rice vinegar or apple
cider vinegar

2 garlic cloves, minced or pressed
(about 2 teaspoons)

1 tablespoon minced fresh ginger

1 teaspoon Tabasco sauce

5 tablespoons (about) hot water

24 cups water

12 ounces spaghetti

1 tablespoon salt

2 tablespoons Asian sesame oil

1 1/2 pounds boneless skinless
chicken breasts

4 scallions or green onions,
cut diagonally into thin slices

1 carrot, grated

Toast the sesame seeds in a medium skillet over medium heat for 10 minutes or until fragrant, stirring frequently. Remove to a plate to cool. Reserve 1 tablespoon of the sesame seeds. Process the remaining sesame seeds, the soy sauce, peanut butter, brown sugar, vinegar, garlic, ginger and hot sauce in a blender or food processor for 30 seconds or until puréed. Add the hot water 1 tablespoon at a time, processing constantly until the sauce has the consistency of heavy cream.

Bring 24 cups water to a boil in a large stockpot over high heat. Add the spaghetti and salt and boil for 10 minutes or until the spaghetti is tender. Drain in a colander and rinse with cold water until cool to the touch; drain again. Toss the spaghetti with the sesame oil in a large bowl until coated.

Arrange the chicken on a broiler rack in a broiler pan sprayed with nonstick cooking spray. Broil 6 inches from the heat source for 4 to 8 minutes or until light brown. Turn the chicken and broil for 6 to 8 minutes longer or until the thickest portion of the chicken is no longer pink and a meat thermometer registers 165 degrees. Remove the chicken to a cutting board and let rest for 5 minutes. Using two forks, shred the chicken into bite-size pieces. Add the chicken, peanut butter sauce, scallions and carrot to the spaghetti mixture and mix well. Sprinkle with the reserved sesame seeds and serve immediately.

Yield: 6 servings

Nutrients Per Serving: Cal 507; Cal from Fat 141; T Fat 15.6 g; Saturated Fat 2.6 g; 27.8% Cal from Fat; Chol 65 mg; Sod 426 mg; T Carbo 53.6 g; 42.3% Cal from Carbo; Fiber 3.1 g; Prot 38 g; 30% Cal from Prot

Chicken Cheese Stacks

3 (8-ounce) boneless skinless
    chicken breasts
3 tablespoons all-purpose flour
1/4 teaspoon salt
3 tablespoons butter
8 ounces mozzarella cheese, sliced
1/2 tablespoon butter
8 ounces mushrooms, sliced

1 tablespoon all-purpose flour
1/8 teaspoon pepper
1/2 cup water
1/2 cup milk
1/4 cup dry white wine (optional)
1 chicken bouillon cube
Sprigs of parsley for garnish

Cut each chicken breast into four equal cutlets. Pound the cutlets 1/8 inch thick between sheets of waxed paper using a meat mallet. Mix 3 tablespoons flour and the salt on a sheet of waxed paper. Coat the cutlets with the flour mixture.

Melt 3 tablespoons butter in a 12-inch skillet over medium heat. Cook the cutlets in batches in the butter until light brown on both sides. Remove the cutlets to a platter, reserving the pan drippings. Arrange the cheese on six of the cutlets and top with the remaining cutlets. Secure with wooden picks.

Heat 1/2 tablespoon butter with the reserved pan drippings and add the mushrooms. Cook until the mushrooms are tender, stirring frequently. Stir in 1 tablespoon flour and the pepper. Gradually add the water, milk, wine and bouillon cube and bring to a boil, stirring constantly to dislodge any browned bits from the bottom of the skillet. Return the chicken stacks to the skillet and reduce the heat to low.

Simmer for 5 minutes or until the cheese melts. Discard the wooden picks and arrange the chicken stacks on a large serving platter. Drizzle with the mushroom sauce and garnish with sprigs of parsley.

Yield: 6 servings

 Nutrients Per Serving: Cal 340; Cal from Fat 162; T Fat 18 g; Saturated Fat 10.7 g; 47.7% Cal from Fat; Chol 118 mg; Sod 549 mg; T Carbo 7.8 g; 9.2% Cal from Carbo; Fiber 0.6 g; Prot 36.6 g; 43.1% Cal from Prot

Chicken Paprikash

8 (6-ounce) bone-in chicken thighs,
  excess fat and skin trimmed
Salt and freshly ground pepper to
  taste
1 teaspoon vegetable oil
1 large onion, cut into halves and
  thinly sliced
1 large red bell pepper, cut into
  1/4-inch strips
1 large green bell pepper, cut into
  1/4-inch strips

3 tablespoons sweet paprika
1 tablespoon all-purpose flour
1/4 teaspoon dried marjoram
1/2 cup dry white wine
1 (14-ounce) can diced
  tomatoes, drained
1 teaspoon salt
1/3 cup sour cream
11/2 teaspoons sweet paprika
2 tablespoons chopped fresh parsley

Adjust the oven rack to the lower-middle position. Season the chicken with salt and pepper to taste. Heat the oil in a large Dutch oven or heavy ovenproof saucepan over medium-high heat for 2 minutes or until shimmering but not smoking. Arrange four of the chicken thighs skin side down in the hot oil and cook for 5 minutes or until the skin is brown and crisp. Turn the chicken with tongs and cook for 5 minutes longer or until brown on the remaining side. Remove the chicken to a platter, reserving the pan drippings. Repeat the process with the remaining chicken thighs and remove to the platter, reserving 1 tablespoon of the pan drippings. Cool the chicken and then remove the skin.

Cook the onion in the reserved pan drippings over medium heat for 5 minutes or until tender. Add the bell peppers and cook for 3 minutes or until the onion is brown and the bell peppers are tender. Mix in 3 tablespoons paprika, the flour and marjoram and cook for 1 minute or until fragrant, stirring occasionally. Add the wine and heat, stirring constantly to dislodge any browned bits from the bottom of the Dutch oven. Stir in the tomatoes and 1 teaspoon salt. Add the chicken and any accumulated juices and bring to a simmer.

Bake, covered, at 300 degrees for 30 minutes or until the chicken is cooked through. The stew may be cooled to room temperature at this point and stored, covered, in the refrigerator for up to 3 days. Bring to a simmer over medium-low heat before proceeding with the recipe.

Mix the sour cream and 1¹/2 teaspoons paprika in a small bowl. Arrange two chicken thighs on each of four serving plates, reserving the pan sauce. Stir a few tablespoons of the sauce into the sour cream mixture and then stir the sour cream mixture into the sauce. Spoon evenly over the chicken and sprinkle with the parsley. Serve immediately.

Yield: 4 servings

Nutrients Per Serving: Cal 499; Cal from Fat 289; T Fat 32.1 g; Saturated Fat 10.1 g; 57.9% Cal from Fat; Chol 152 mg; Sod 864 mg; T Carbo 19.1 g; 15.3% Cal from Carbo; Fiber 4.5 g; Prot 33.4 g; 26.8% Cal from Prot

Oriental Chicken

4 (3-ounce) packages Oriental
   ramen noodles
2 cups water
3 tablespoons margarine

8 ounces cooked chicken, chopped
¹/2 teaspoon ginger
1 (10-ounce) package broccoli florets
2 cups grated carrots

Reserve the seasoning packets and break the noodles. Combine the noodles, the contents of 1 reserved seasoning packet and the water in a saucepan and cook for 3 minutes; drain. Cover to keep warm.

Heat the margarine in a skillet or wok and add the contents of the remaining reserved seasoning packets, the chicken and ginger. Sauté until heated through and stir in the broccoli and carrots. Cook until the vegetables are tender, stirring frequently. Serve with the noodles.

Yield: 4 servings

Nutrients Per Serving: Cal 613; Cal from Fat 251; T Fat 27.7 g; Saturated Fat 8.8 g; 40.9% Cal from Fat; Chol 48 mg; Sod 1153 mg; T Carbo 63.4 g; 41.4% Cal from Carbo; Fiber 2.6 g; Prot 27.1 g; 17.7% Cal from Prot

Stuffing-Topped Chicken and Broccoli

1 (6-ounce) package stuffing mix
2 (10-ounce) cans cream of
    chicken soup
1 cup water
3 tablespoons sour cream

3¹/₂ cups chopped cooked chicken
2 (10-ounce) packages frozen broccoli
    florets, thawed and drained
2 cups cooked instant white rice

Prepare the stuffing mix using the package directions; do not bake. Combine the soup, water and sour cream in a bowl and mix well. Stir in the chicken, broccoli and rice.

Spoon the chicken mixture into a greased 3-quart baking dish and spread the stuffing mixture over the top. Bake, covered, at 350 degrees for 30 minutes. Remove the cover and bake for 15 to 20 minutes longer or until bubbly.

Yield: 8 servings

 Nutrients Per Serving: Cal 545; Cal from Fat 76; T Fat 8.4 g; Saturated Fat 2.5 g; 13.9% Cal from Fat; Chol 60 mg; Sod 961 mg; T Carbo 90.8 g; 66.6% Cal from Carbo; Fiber 3 g; Prot 26.5 g; 19.4% Cal from Prot

TO INCREASE FIBER INTAKE, USE CRUSHED
BRAN PRODUCTS AS A CRUNCHY TOPPING FOR CASSEROLES,
SALADS, OR COOKED VEGETABLES.

Ground Chicken Patties

20 ounces ground chicken
2/3 cup instant potato flakes
1 egg, lightly beaten
1 to 2 tablespoons ranch salad dressing
Salt and pepper to taste
Vegetable oil for frying
Chopped fresh parsley for garnish

Combine the ground chicken, potato flakes, egg and salad dressing in a bowl and mix well. Season with salt and pepper.

Shape the ground chicken mixture into four patties. Fry in oil in a skillet until brown on both sides, turning once; drain. Arrange the patties on a platter and sprinkle with parsley.

Note: You may substitute ground turkey for the ground chicken, 1 cup of bread crumbs for the potato flakes and nonstick cooking spray for the oil.

Yield: 4 servings

Nutrients Per Serving: Cal 327; Cal from Fat 178; T Fat 19.7 g; Saturated Fat 4.8 g; 54.5% Cal from Fat; Chol 174 mg; Sod 202 mg; T Carbo 8.4 g; 10.3% Cal from Carbo; Fiber 0.6 g; Prot 28.8 g; 35.3% Cal from Prot. *Nutritional profile does not include oil for frying.*

Turkey Fillets with Peach Sauce

4 (4-ounce) turkey tenderloins
1 (10-ounce) can cream of chicken soup
1/2 cup chicken broth
1/2 cup orange juice
3 tablespoons peach preserves
6 large fresh mushrooms, cut into 1/4-inch slices
Hot cooked rice

Arrange the turkey in a single layer in a 2-quart baking dish. Combine the soup, broth, orange juice and preserves in a bowl and mix well. Stir in the mushrooms. Spoon over the turkey and bake, covered, at 350 degrees for 1 hour. Serve over hot cooked rice, if desired.

Yield: 4 servings

Nutrients Per Serving: Cal 273; Cal from Fat 72; T Fat 8 g; Saturated Fat 2.4 g; Chol 80 mg; Sod 840 mg; T Carbo 20.8 g; Fiber 1.1 g; Prot 29.5 g

Seafood

Peptic Ulcer Disease

Not all individuals with a "stomach ache" have a peptic ulcer. However, in the United States, ulcers remain a common cause of upper abdominal pain. Peptic ulcers are a defect in the lining of the stomach or duodenum (first portion of the small intestine). Epigastric pain is the presenting symptom in 80 to 90 percent of cases. The pain may be precipitated by food (in gastric ulcers) or partially relieved by food (in duodenal ulcers). In most cases, the cause of peptic ulcers is due to an infection (helicobacter pylori) or medication (nonsteroidal anti-inflammatory medications or aspirin). Rarely is an ulcer cancerous.

Peptic ulcers can be most efficiently diagnosed by an upper endoscopy (EGD), which allows direct visualization of the lining of the stomach and the ability to obtain a biopsy. The specimen is tested for infection or cancer. Once the cause of the peptic ulcers is determined, treatment may include an antibiotic for infection, medication to decrease stomach acid, or surgery, if cancerous.

All individuals should be encouraged to eat a balanced diet. Smoking should be discouraged, as it can delay ulcer healing and increase the likelihood of recurrence. American folklore has suggested that a poor diet is a cause of ulcers. While there is no scientific proof that any specific food causes ulcers, a well-balanced diet is still the best medicine.

Flounder in Lemon Dill Sauce

1 onion, thinly sliced
3 tablespoons butter
1 tablespoon chopped fresh dill weed, or
    3/4 teaspoon dried dill weed
1 tablespoon lemon juice
4 (4-ounce) flounder fillets
Lemon slices for garnish

Combine the onion, butter, dill weed and lemon juice in a 10-inch skillet. Cook over medium-low heat until the butter melts and is hot.

Add the fillets. Cook, covered, for 8 to 10 minutes or until the fillets flake easily when tested with a fork, basting frequently with the lemon dill sauce. Arrange the fillets on a heated deep serving platter and drizzle with the sauce. Garnish with lemon slices.

Yield: 4 servings

 Nutrients Per Serving: Cal 189; Cal from Fat 90; T Fat 9.9 g; Saturated Fat 5.7 g; 47.7% Cal from Fat; Chol 79 mg; Sod 181 mg; T Carbo 2.9 g; 6.1% Cal from Carbo; Fiber 0.5 g; Prot 21.8 g; 46.2% Cal from Prot

Neptune's Flounder

4 (4-ounce) flounder fillets
1 (10-ounce) can cream of shrimp soup
1 (4-ounce) can small or tiny shrimp,
   drained and chopped

40 butter crackers, crushed
1/2 cup (1 stick) butter, melted

Arrange the fillets in a single layer in a shallow baking dish. Spread the soup over the fillets and sprinkle with the shrimp.

Toss the cracker crumbs and butter in a bowl until coated and sprinkle over the top. Bake at 350 degrees for 30 to 40 minutes or until bubbly and the fillets flake easily when tested with a fork.

Yield: 4 servings

Nutrients Per Serving: Cal 557; Cal from Fat 330; T Fat 36.7 g; Saturated Fat 18.6 g; 59.3% Cal from Fat; Chol 176 mg; Sod 1195 mg; T Carbo 24.9 g; 17.9% Cal from Carbo; Fiber 0.1 g; Prot 31.8 g; 22.8% Cal from Prot

Broiled Haddock

16 ounces frozen
   haddock fillets
3 tablespoons margarine

3 tablespoons lemon juice
1 tablespoon seasoned salt

Arrange the frozen fillets on a sheet of foil large enough to enclose. Dot the fillets evenly with the margarine and drizzle with the lemon juice. Sprinkle with the seasoned salt. Fold the foil over the fillets and seal tightly.

Bake at 400 degrees for 1 hour. Open the foil and broil for 2 minutes. Serve immediately. Note: Icelandic flounder is also recommended.

Yield: 4 servings

Nutrients Per Serving: Cal 174; Cal from Fat 84; T Fat 9.3 g; Saturated Fat 1.6 g; 48.2% Cal from Fat; Chol 65 mg; Sod 1945 mg; T Carbo 1.1 g; 2.5% Cal from Carbo; Fiber 0 g; Prot 21.5 g; 49.3% Cal from Prot

Poor Man's Lobster

2 cups water
1 tablespoon Old Bay seasoning
1 tablespoon vinegar
1 teaspoon salt

16 ounces frozen haddock or cod
   fillets, cut into bite-size pieces
Melted butter or margarine (optional)

Combine the water, Old Bay seasoning, vinegar and salt in a saucepan and bring to a boil. Add the haddock and reduce the heat.

Simmer for 15 to 20 minutes or until the haddock flakes easily, stirring occasionally. Drain and serve with melted butter.

Note: For a spicier flavor, add additional Old Bay seasoning.

Yield: 4 servings

Nutrients Per Serving: Cal 93; Cal from Fat 7; T Fat 0.8 g; Saturated Fat 0.1 g; 7.5% Cal from Fat; Chol 65 mg; Sod 1161 mg; T Carbo 0.2 g; 0.9% Cal from Carbo; Fiber 0 g; Prot 21.4 g; 91.6% Cal from Prot
Nutritional profile includes the vinegar mixture.

Salmon with Garlic and Dill

4 (5-ounce) salmon fillets,
   3/4 inch thick
3 or 4 garlic cloves, pressed
Salt and pepper to taste

1 cup chopped dill weed
1/2 cup plain yogurt
1/2 cup sour cream
1 tablespoon Dijon mustard

Arrange the fillets in a single layer in a buttered baking dish. Bake at 375 degrees for 20 minutes. Sprinkle with the garlic, salt and pepper.

Combine the dill weed, yogurt, sour cream and Dijon mustard in a bowl and mix well. Spread over the fillets and bake for 5 minutes longer.

Yield: 4 servings

Nutrients Per Serving: Cal 367; Cal from Fat 232; T Fat 25.8 g; Saturated Fat 7.9 g; 63.2% Cal from Fat; Chol 101 mg; Sod 114 mg; T Carbo 3.3 g; 3.6% Cal from Carbo; Fiber 0 g; Prot 30.4 g; 33.2% Cal from Prot

Salmon Cakes

1 (14-ounce) can salmon, drained
and flaked
1/4 cup milk

1 egg, lightly beaten
2 cups seasoned bread crumbs, or
1 sleeve of crackers, crushed

Combine the salmon, milk and egg in a bowl and mix well. Stir in 1 cup of the bread crumbs. Gradually add the remaining bread crumbs, stirring constantly until the mixture adheres. If the salmon mixture is too moist the cakes will not adhere, and if the mixture is too dry the cakes will crumble.

Shape the salmon mixture into five cakes and arrange on a baking sheet. Broil for 5 to 8 minutes per side or until golden brown. You may panfry the cakes, if desired.

Yield: 5 cakes

 Nutrients Per Serving: Cal 310; Cal from Fat 74; T Fat 8.2 g; Saturated Fat 2 g; 23.8% Cal from Fat; Chol 78 mg; Sod 1717 mg; T Carbo 34.5 g; 44.5% Cal from Carbo; Fiber 2 g; Prot 24.6 g; 31.7% Cal from Prot

Slammin' Salmon Cakes

1/2 Vidalia onion, chopped
1 tablespoon olive oil
1 (16-ounce) can salmon, drained
and flaked
1/2 cup all-purpose flour

1/8 teaspoon pepper
3/4 cup milk
1 egg, lightly beaten
Olive oil for frying

Cook the onion in 1 tablespoon olive oil in a skillet until the onion is caramelized. Mix the salmon, flour and pepper in a bowl. Stir in the onion, milk and egg; the mixture will be of a paste consistency. Shape into eight cakes.

Add enough olive oil to a 10-inch skillet to measure 1 inch and heat until hot. Add the cakes to the hot oil and cook until golden brown on both sides; drain.

Yield: 8 cakes

 Nutrients Per Serving: Cal 152; Cal from Fat 63; T Fat 6.9 g; Saturated Fat 1.6 g; 41.4% Cal from Fat; Chol 53 mg; Sod 324 mg; T Carbo 8.2 g; 21.6% Cal from Carbo; Fiber 0.2 g; Prot 14.1 g; 37.1% Cal from Prot. *Nutritional profile does not include olive oil for frying.*

Salmon Divan

4 (10-ounce) packages frozen broccoli
1/4 cup (1/2 stick) butter or margarine
1/4 cup all-purpose flour
1 teaspoon salt
1/4 teaspoon pepper
2 cups milk, heated
2 tablespoons lemon juice
4 cups canned salmon or poached fresh salmon
1/4 cup grated Parmesan cheese
1 tablespoon dry fine bread crumbs

Cook the broccoli using the package directions; drain. Melt the butter in a saucepan and stir in the flour, salt and pepper. Cook until bubbly and stir in the milk. Cook over medium heat until smooth and thickened and of a sauce consistency, stirring constantly. Remove from the heat and stir in the lemon juice.

Layer the salmon and broccoli in a 9×13-inch baking dish. Pour the sauce over the top. Toss the cheese and bread crumbs in a bowl and sprinkle over the top. Bake at 450 degrees for 15 to 20 minutes or until golden brown and bubbly.

Yield: 8 servings

Nutrients Per Serving: Cal 304; Cal from Fat 128; T Fat 14.2 g; Saturated Fat 6 g; 42.2% Cal from Fat; Chol 82 mg; Sod 1057 mg; T Carbo 14.4 g; 19% Cal from Carbo; Fiber 4.4 g; Prot 29.5 g; 38.9% Cal from Prot

Salmon Loaf

1 (16-ounce) can salmon, drained
and flaked
2 1/2 cups bread crumbs
1 (10-ounce) can cream celery soup
2 eggs, beaten
1 cup heavy cream

1 tablespoon pickle relish
1/4 teaspoon Old Bay seasoning
1/4 teaspoon onion powder
1 hard-cooked egg, chopped for
garnish

Combine the salmon, bread crumbs, soup and two beaten eggs in a bowl and mix well. Shape into a loaf in a greased 5×9-inch loaf pan. Bake at 350 degrees for 1 hour.

Combine the cream, pickle relish, Old Bay seasoning and onion powder in a bowl and mix until of a sauce consistency. Remove the loaf to a platter and drizzle with the sauce. Garnish with the hard-cooked egg.

Yield: 6 servings

 Nutrients Per Serving: Cal 483; Cal from Fat 232; T Fat 25.7 g; Saturated Fat 11.4 g; 48% Cal from Fat; Chol 160 mg; Sod 1237 mg; T Carbo 38.2 g; 31.6% Cal from Carbo; Fiber 1.4 g; Prot 24.6 g; 20.4% Cal from Prot

Imitation Crab Cakes

1/2 cup mayonnaise
1 envelope Old Bay Crab Cake Classic seasoning
1 pound fresh trout, flaked

Combine the mayonnaise and seasoning in a bowl and mix well. Add the trout and toss gently until coated.

Shape into six cakes. Broil or panfry the cakes for 4 to 5 minutes per side or until golden brown; drain.

Yield: 6 cakes

 Nutrients Per Serving: Cal 196; Cal from Fat 145; T Fat 16 g; Saturated Fat 2.8 g; 74.1% Cal from Fat; Chol 70 mg; Sod 824 mg; T Carbo 0 g; 0% Cal from Carbo; Fiber 0 g; Prot 12.7 g; 25.9% Cal from Prot

Creamy Tuna Fettuccini

*4 cups broccoli florets, or
    1 (16-ounce) package frozen chopped broccoli
8 ounces fettuccini
1 (12-ounce) can tuna, drained and flaked
1 cup ricotta cheese
1/2 cup milk
1/4 cup (1 ounce) grated Parmesan cheese
1/2 teaspoon garlic salt
1/2 teaspoon Italian seasoning
Salt and pepper to taste*

Cook the broccoli in boiling water in a large saucepan until tender. Remove the broccoli to a serving bowl using a slotted spoon, reserving the liquid. Add the pasta to the reserved liquid and cook until tender; drain. Add the pasta to the broccoli and mix gently. Stir in the tuna.

Combine the ricotta cheese, milk, Parmesan cheese, garlic salt, Italian seasoning, salt and pepper in the same saucepan and mix well. Cook over medium heat until blended, stirring occasionally. Pour over the pasta mixture and toss to coat.

Yield: 4 servings

Nutrients Per Serving: Cal 496; Cal from Fat 130; T Fat 14.4 g; Saturated Fat 7.4 g; 26.2% Cal from Fat; Chol 74 mg; Sod 493 mg; T Carbo 50.5 g; 40.8% Cal from Carbo; Fiber 5.4 g; Prot 40.9 g; 33% Cal from Prot. *Nutritional profile does not include Italian seasoning.*

Baked Tuna Supreme

1 (10-ounce) package frozen
   chopped broccoli
1 (9-ounce) can tuna, drained
   and flaked
1 (10-ounce) can cream of
   mushroom soup

1/2 cup (2 ounces) shredded sharp
   Cheddar cheese
1/4 cup milk
1 cup soft bread crumbs
1 tablespoon butter or
   margarine, melted

Cook the broccoli using the package directions; drain. Spread the broccoli in a 7x10-inch baking dish and top with the tuna.

Combine the soup, cheese and milk in a saucepan and cook until the cheese melts, stirring occasionally. Spoon the soup mixture over the prepared layers. Toss the bread crumbs and butter in a bowl to coat and sprinkle over the top. Bake at 350 degrees for 20 to 25 minutes or until heated through.

Yield: 6 servings

Nutrients Per Serving: Cal 253; Cal from Fat 105; T Fat 11.7 g; Saturated Fat 5.1 g; 41.6% Cal from Fat; Chol 37 mg; Sod 607 mg; T Carbo 19.5 g; 30.9% Cal from Carbo; Fiber 1.9 g; Prot 17.4 g; 27.6% Cal from Prot

Crab Cakes

8 ounces crab meat, drained and flaked
1 egg, lightly beaten
1/4 cup dry bread crumbs
2 tablespoons mayonnaise

1 teaspoon Worcestershire sauce
1/2 teaspoon dry mustard
1/4 teaspoon paprika
3 to 4 tablespoons butter

Mix the crab meat, egg, bread crumbs, mayonnaise, Worcestershire sauce, mustard and paprika in a bowl. Shape into six cakes. Heat the butter in a skillet until melted. Panfry the cakes in the butter until brown on all sides; drain.

Yield: 6 cakes

Nutrients Per Serving: Cal 162; Cal from Fat 113; T Fat 12.5 g; Saturated Fat 5.8 g; 69.8% Cal from Fat; Chol 87 mg; Sod 279 mg; T Carbo 3.6 g; 8.9% Cal from Carbo; Fiber 0.1 g; Prot 8.6 g; 21.3% Cal from Prot

Crab Melt-a-Ways

1 (7-ounce) can white crab meat,
   drained and flaked
1 (5-ounce) jar Old English
   cheese spread

1/2 cup (1 stick) butter, melted
1/2 teaspoon garlic powder
1/2 teaspoon Old Bay seasoning
6 English muffins, split

Combine the crab meat, cheese spread, butter, garlic powder and Old Bay seasoning in a bowl and mix well. Spread on the cut sides of the muffins.

Arrange the muffin halves crab side up on a baking sheet. Broil until bubbly. Cut each half into quarters. Serve warm.

Yield: 6 servings

Nutrients Per Serving: Cal 373; Cal from Fat 197; T Fat 21.8 g; Saturated Fat 13 g; 52.9% Cal from Fat; Chol 88 mg; Sod 914 mg; T Carbo 27.7 g; 29.7% Cal from Carbo; Fiber 2 g; Prot 16.2 g; 17.4% Cal from Prot

Scalloped Oysters

2 pints oysters
2 sleeves butter crackers or club
   crackers, crushed (about 4 cups)
1 cup (2 sticks) butter, melted

Pepper to taste
1 1/2 cups light cream
1 teaspoon salt
1/2 teaspoon Worcestershire sauce

Drain the oysters, reserving 1/2 cup of the liquor. Toss the cracker crumbs and butter in a bowl until coated.

Spread one-third of the crumb mixture in the bottom of an 8×12-inch baking dish. Top with half the oysters. Sprinkle with pepper. Top with half the remaining crumb mixture and the remaining oysters. Sprinkle with pepper.

Combine the reserved liquor, the cream, salt and Worcestershire sauce in a bowl and mix well. Pour over the prepared layers and sprinkle with the remaining crumb mixture. Bake at 350 degrees for 50 minutes.

Yield: 8 servings

Nutrients Per Serving: Cal 499; Cal from Fat 375; T Fat 41.7 g; Saturated Fat 21.7 g; 75.2% Cal from Fat; Chol 120 mg; Sod 871 mg; T Carbo 20.6 g; 16.5% Cal from Carbo; Fiber 0 g; Prot 10.4 g; 8.3% Cal from Prot

Easy Baked Shrimp

1/4 cup canola oil
1 1/2 pounds peeled deveined shrimp
1 tablespoon jarred minced garlic
1/2 teaspoon salt
1/4 teaspoon freshly ground pepper
1/2 cup Italian-seasoned bread crumbs
3 tablespoons chopped fresh parsley

Pour the canola oil into a 9×13-inch baking dish. Add the shrimp and stir until coated. Sprinkle with the garlic, salt and pepper. Add the bread crumbs and parsley and toss to coat.

Bake at 475 degrees for 5 minutes. Gently turn the shrimp with a slotted spatula and bake for 3 to 5 minutes longer or until the shrimp turn pink and the bread crumbs are brown. Serve with lemon wedges and hot cooked rice.

Yield: 6 servings

Nutrients Per Serving: Cal 196; Cal from Fat 84; T Fat 9.4 g; Saturated Fat 0.7 g; 42.9% Cal from Fat; Chol 120 mg; Sod 752 mg; T Carbo 8.2 g; 16.8% Cal from Carbo; Fiber 0.6 g; Prot 19.7 g; 40.3% Cal from Prot

Grilled Shrimp in Peanut Sauce

1/4 cup creamy peanut butter
1/4 cup soy sauce
1/4 cup sugar
3 garlic cloves, minced
2 tablespoons vegetable oil
1 tablespoon water
1 1/2 pounds shrimp, peeled and deveined

Combine the peanut butter and 2 tablespoons of the soy sauce in a saucepan and mix well. Stir in the remaining 2 tablespoons soy sauce, the sugar, garlic, oil and water. Cook until the sugar dissolves, stirring occasionally. Thread the shrimp on water-soaked bamboo skewers or metal skewers and brush with the peanut sauce. Grill, with the lid closed, over medium heat for 5 to 6 minutes or until the shrimp turn pink, turning halfway through the grilling process. Bring the remaining peanut sauce to a boil and boil for 2 minutes. Brush the grilled shrimp with the remaining sauce before serving.

Yield: 4 servings

Nutrients Per Serving: Cal 343; Cal from Fat 161; T Fat 17.9 g; Saturated Fat 3.2 g; 46.9% Cal from Fat; Chol 255 mg; Sod 1351 mg; T Carbo 6.4 g; 7.5% Cal from Carbo; Fiber 1.1 g; Prot 39.1 g; 45.6% Cal from Prot

Shrimp and Grits

Grits

1 (24-ounce) package grits
1 cup chopped green onions
2 tablespoons extra-virgin olive oil
1 cup (4 ounces) shredded sharp
    Cheddar cheese
1/2 to 1 cup heavy cream
1/2 cup chopped tomatoes
2 tablespoons butter

Shrimp Sauce

1/2 onion, chopped
2 tablespoons butter
1 pound shrimp, peeled and deveined
1/2 cup (2 ounces) shredded
    Parmesan cheese
1/2 cup fresh spinach, finely chopped
    (optional)
Juice of 1 lemon
1/4 cup heavy cream

To prepare the grits, cook the grits using the package directions. Remove from the heat and cover to keep warm. Sauté the green onions in the olive oil in a skillet until tender. Stir the green onions, cheese, cream, tomatoes and butter into the grits. Cook over medium heat until the cheese melts, stirring occasionally.

To prepare the sauce, sauté the onion in the butter in a saucepan until tender. Stir in the shrimp, cheese, spinach, lemon juice and cream and mix well. Bring to a boil and cook until the shrimp turn pink and the cheese melts. Spoon the sauce evenly over the grits on four serving plates. Serve immediately.

Yield: 4 servings

 Nutrients Per Serving: Cal 1367; Cal from Fat 570; T Fat 63.4 g; Saturated Fat 34.6 g; 41.7% Cal from Fat; Chol 343 mg; Sod 763 mg; T Carbo 145.6 g; 42.6% Cal from Carbo; Fiber 4.1 g; Prot 53.7 g; 15.7% Cal from Prot

Shrimp in White Wine Saffron Sauce

24 large shrimp, peeled and deveined
3 garlic cloves, sliced
Salt and white pepper to taste
2 tablespoons olive oil
1/2 cup finely chopped red onion
1 cup organic chicken stock or
    low-sodium chicken broth
3/4 cup light cream
1/4 cup Italian white table wine

1/2 teaspoon saffron threads
6 ounces mascarpone cheese
1 tablespoon olive oil
1 (14-ounce) can hearts of palm,
    drained and chopped into
    1-inch pieces
Hot cooked linguini, angel hair pasta
    or white rice

Arrange the shrimp in a shallow dish and sprinkle with the garlic, salt and white pepper. Marinate, covered, in the refrigerator for 2 hours or longer.

Remove the garlic from the shrimp and sauté the garlic in 2 tablespoons olive oil in a skillet until golden brown. Discard the garlic, reserving the olive oil. Add the onion to the reserved olive oil and cook for 5 minutes or until the onion is tender. Stir in the stock, cream, wine and saffron. Cook over medium heat for 10 minutes. Stir in the cheese and simmer over low heat until thickened and of a sauce consistency, stirring frequently.

Sauté the shrimp in 1 tablespoon olive oil in a saucepan for 3 minutes or just until the shrimp turn pink; drain. Stir the shrimp into the saffron sauce and simmer over low heat for 5 minutes. Stir in the hearts of palm and simmer for 1 minute. Remove from the heat and cover. Serve over hot cooked linguini, angel hair pasta or white rice.

Note: Serve with Oregon pinot gris, French vouvray, or California sauvignon blanc.

Yield: 4 servings

 Nutrients Per Serving: Cal 469; Cal from Fat 360; T Fat 40 g; Saturated Fat 17.7 g; 76.8% Cal from Fat; Chol 155 mg; Sod 677 mg; T Carbo 9.6 g; 8.2% Cal from Carbo; Fiber 2.8 g; Prot 17.6 g; 15% Cal from Prot

Seafood Pasta Delight

8 ounces vermicelli	1 red bell pepper, julienned
2 tablespoons cornstarch	1 yellow bell pepper, julienned
1 teaspoon sugar	1 cup snow peas
1/8 teaspoon salt	2 or 3 garlic cloves, minced
1/8 teaspoon pepper	1/4 teaspoon ginger
1/2 cup chicken broth	1 tablespoon olive oil
1/2 cup dry white wine or	1 pound shrimp, peeled and deveined
chicken broth	1 pound sea scallops, cut into halves
1/4 cup soy sauce	2 teaspoons sesame oil

Cook the pasta using the package directions and drain. Cover to keep warm. Combine the cornstarch, sugar, salt and pepper in a bowl and mix well. Stir in the broth, wine and soy sauce.

Stir-fry the bell peppers, snow peas, garlic and ginger in the olive oil in a nonstick skillet or wok for 2 to 4 minutes or until the bell peppers and snow peas are tender-crisp. Add the shrimp and scallops and stir-fry for 2 minutes longer. Stir in the cornstarch mixture and bring to a boil.

Cook for 2 minutes or until thickened, stirring constantly. Mix in the pasta and cook until the scallops are firm and opaque and the shrimp turn pink. Drizzle with the sesame oil and serve immediately.

Yield: 8 servings

Nutrients Per Serving: Cal 276; Cal from Fat 45; T Fat 5.1 g; Saturated Fat 0.6 g; 16.3% Cal from Fat; Chol 104 mg; Sod 792 mg; T Carbo 31.2 g; 45.2% Cal from Carbo; Fiber 2.3 g; Prot 26.6 g; 38.5% Cal from Prot

Sweets

Fiber

Fiber comes in many forms, and, while it may be very confusing, it is the intake of **Total Fiber** that is crucial. Each recipe contains an analysis of the Total Fiber per serving. The minimum recommended daily fiber intake is from twenty grams for females to thirty-five grams for males.

The two types of fiber mentioned most frequently are **soluble** which dissolves in water, and **insoluble,** which does not. Foods that are sources of soluble fiber include oatmeal, beans, peas, citrus fruits, apples, and strawberries. Soluble fiber binds with LDL ("bad" cholesterol) and helps prevent cardiovascular disease. Soluble fiber also slows the absorption of sugar and decreases blood sugar levels in diabetic conditions.

Insoluble fiber, such as that found in wheat bran, whole wheat bread, bananas, cabbage, beets, carrots, and tomatoes, absorbs water. Fiber can absorb up to thirty times its weight in water. The bulk that forms when insoluble fiber is ingested helps with digestion and the elimination of food. This can be very beneficial in the treatment of numerous gastrointestinal conditions. When starting an increased fiber diet, begin gradually or you may experience increased flatus, bloating, or cramping.

Hugs and Kisses

1 (16-ounce) package miniature pretzels
1 (12-ounce) package chocolate
   candy kisses

1 (14-ounce) package "M & M's" Plain
   Chocolate Candies

Arrange the pretzels in a single layer on an ungreased baking sheet. Top each pretzel with one candy kiss. Bake at 275 degrees for 2 to 3 minutes or until the kisses are soft but not melted.

Remove from the oven and immediately place one "M & M" chocolate candy on each kiss. Let stand until cool. Store in the refrigerator to keep from melting, if desired.

Yield: 45 (2-pretzel) servings

Nutrients Per Serving: Cal 126; Cal from Fat 44; T Fat 4.9 g; Saturated Fat 1.3 g; 35% Cal from Fat; Chol 3 mg; Sod 184 mg; T Carbo 18.3 g; 58.3% Cal from Carbo; Fiber 0.7 g; Prot 2.1 g; 6.7% Cal from Prot

Puppy Chow

1/2 cup (1 stick) butter
1 cup smooth peanut butter
2 cups (12 ounces) chocolate chips

1 (12-ounce) package Crispix cereal
3 cups confectioners' sugar

Melt the butter in a large saucepan over low heat, tilting the pan until the side and bottom are coated. Stir in the peanut butter and chocolate chips and cook until blended. Add the cereal and stir to coat.

Pour the confectioners' sugar into a brown bag and add the cereal mixture. Shake until the cereal mixture is coated.

Yield: 12 servings

Nutrients Per Serving: Cal 589; Cal from Fat 252; T Fat 28 g; Saturated Fat 11.2 g; 42.8% Cal from Fat; Chol 21 mg; Sod 413 mg; T Carbo 76.6 g; 52% Cal from Carbo; Fiber 6 g; Prot 7.6 g; 5.2% Cal from Prot

Cheesecake

16 whole graham crackers, crushed
1 cup (2 sticks) butter, melted
24 ounces cream cheese, softened
2 cups sour cream

6 eggs
1¹/₂ cups sugar
1 tablespoon vanilla extract

Mix the graham cracker crumbs and butter by hand in a bowl to coat. Press over the bottom and up the side of a 9-inch springform pan. Combine the remaining ingredients in a mixing bowl. Beat at medium speed until blended, scraping the bowl occasionally. Spoon into the prepared pan.

Bake at 350 degrees for 1 hour. Turn off the oven. Let the cheesecake stand with the door closed for 70 minutes; do not peek. Remove the cheesecake from the oven and let stand until cool. Store, covered, in the refrigerator.

Yield: 12 servings

Nutrients Per Serving: Cal 594; Cal from Fat 418; T Fat 46.5 g; Saturated Fat 27.9 g; 70.4% Cal from Fat; Chol 225 mg; Sod 431 mg; T Carbo 35.2 g; 23.7% Cal from Carbo; Fiber 0 g; Prot 8.8 g; 5.9% Cal from Prot

Berry Cheesecake

2 (3-ounce) packages ladyfingers
2 cups heavy whipping cream
16 ounces cream cheese, softened

2 cups sugar
1 teaspoon vanilla extract
1 pint fresh blueberries or raspberries

Line the bottom and side of a 9-inch springform pan with the ladyfingers. Beat the whipping cream in a mixing bowl until stiff peaks form.

Beat the cream cheese and sugar in a mixing bowl until creamy. Fold the whipped cream and vanilla into the cream cheese mixture and spoon into the prepared pan. Chill, covered, for 2 hours or longer. Top with the blueberries just before serving.

Note: You may substitute any fruit pie filling for the blueberries.

Yield: 8 servings

Nutrients Per Serving: Cal 701; Cal from Fat 385; T Fat 42.8 g; Saturated Fat 26.3 g; 54.9% Cal from Fat; Chol 217 mg; Sod 222 mg; T Carbo 71 g; 40,5% Cal from Carbo; Fiber 1.2 g; Prot 8 g; 4.6% Cal from Prot

Blueberry Pineapple Gelatin Dessert

1 (15-ounce) can juice-pack
    crushed pineapple
2 (3-ounce) packages blueberry or
    blackberry gelatin
2 cups boiling water
1 pint frozen blueberries

8 ounces cream cheese, softened
1 cup sour cream
$1/2$ cup sugar
Chopped nuts for garnish
Grated coconut for garnish

Drain the pineapple, reserving the juice. Add enough water to the reserved juice to measure 1 cup. Dissolve the gelatin in the boiling water in a heatproof bowl. Stir in the pineapple juice mixture, pineapple and blueberries. Pour into a 9×13-inch dish and chill until set. Beat the next three ingredients in a mixing bowl and spread over the chilled layer. Sprinkle with nuts and coconut. Chill, covered, until serving time.

Yield: 12 servings

Nutrients Per Serving: Cal 234; Cal from Fat 96; T Fat 10.8 g; Saturated Fat 6.7 g; 41.1% Cal from Fat; Chol 29 mg; Sod 102 mg; T Carbo 31.1 g; 53.3% Cal from Carbo; Fiber 1 g; Prot 3.3 g; 5.7% Cal from Prot

Coconut Mousse

3 envelopes unflavored gelatin
$1/3$ cup water
2 cups half-and-half
1 cup sugar

2 cups grated coconut
3 cups heavy whipping cream
1 teaspoon coconut extract

Soften the gelatin in the water in a bowl. Bring the half-and-half to a boil in a saucepan. Add the gelatin mixture and sugar and cook until the sugar dissolves, stirring frequently. Let stand until cool and stir in the coconut. Beat the whipping cream and flavoring in a mixing bowl until stiff peaks form. Fold into the coconut mixture. Spoon the mousse into an 8-cup mold. Chill for 1 hour or until set.

Yield: 10 servings

Nutrients Per Serving: Cal 467; Cal from Fat 320; T Fat 35.6 g; Saturated Fat 23.4 g; 68.6% Cal from Fat; Chol 111 mg; Sod 84 mg; T Carbo 31 g; 26.6% Cal from Carbo; Fiber 0.6 g; Prot 5.7 g; 4.9% Cal from Prot. *Nutritional analysis does not include coconut extract.*

Peanut Butter Chocolate Delight

16 chocolate sandwich cookies, crushed
2 tablespoons butter or margarine, melted
8 ounces cream cheese, softened
1 cup confectioners' sugar
1/2 cup peanut butter
16 ounces whipped topping
15 miniature peanut butter cups, chopped
1 cup cold milk
1 (4-ounce) package chocolate fudge instant pudding mix
1/2 cup confectioners' sugar
4 chocolate sandwich cookies, crushed

Toss sixteen crushed cookies with the butter in a bowl until combined. Press over the bottom of an ungreased 9×9-inch dish. Beat the cream cheese, 1 cup confectioners' sugar and the peanut butter in a mixing bowl until smooth. Fold in half the whipped topping. Spread the peanut butter mixture in the prepared dish and sprinkle with the peanut butter cups.

Beat the milk, pudding mix and 1/2 cup confectioners' sugar in a mixing bowl at low speed for 2 minutes. Fold in the remaining whipped topping and spread over the prepared layers. Sprinkle with four crushed cookies. Chill, covered, for 3 hours or longer.

Yield: 8 servings

 Nutrients Per Serving: Cal 716; Cal from Fat 385; T Fat 42.9 g; Saturated Fat 21.2 g; 53.8% Cal from Fat; Chol 84 mg; Sod 641 mg; T Carbo 70.8 g; 39.6% Cal from Carbo; Fiber 2.1 g; Prot 11.9 g; 6.6% Cal from Prot

Grape Nut Pudding

2 (4-ounce) packages vanilla instant
    pudding mix
3 cups milk

8 ounces whipped topping
1 cup Grape-Nuts cereal

Combine the pudding mix and milk in a mixing bowl and beat until the pudding begins to thicken. Fold in the whipping topping and then stir in the cereal. Chill, covered, for 24 hours before serving to allow the cereal to soften.

Note: You may substitute with sugar-free vanilla instant pudding mix.

Yield: 8 servings

Nutrients Per Serving: Cal 282; Cal from Fat 68; T Fat 7.5 g; Saturated Fat 5.9 g; 24.1% Cal from Fat; Chol 7 mg; Sod 543 mg; T Carbo 48.8 g; 69.3% Cal from Carbo; Fiber 1.2 g; Prot 4.6 g; 6.5% Cal from Prot

Munty Sweet Yogurt

2 (12-ounce) cans evaporated milk
1 cup plain yogurt

1 cup sugar

Bring the evaporated milk to a boil in a saucepan. Remove from the heat and let stand until room temperature. Beat the yogurt in a mixing bowl until fluffy. Stir in the evaporated milk and sugar.

Pour into a baking dish. Bake at 150 to 200 degrees for 4 to 5 hours or until thickened and solid. Chill, covered, for 1 hour or longer before serving. Serve chilled.

Yield: 6 servings

Nutrients Per Serving: Cal 312; Cal from Fat 89; T Fat 9.9 g; Saturated Fat 6.1 g; 28.5% Cal from Fat; Chol 38 mg; Sod 139 mg; T Carbo 46.6 g; 59.8% Cal from Carbo; Fiber 0 g; Prot 9.1 g; 11.7% Cal from Prot

Prize Peach Cobbler

2 cups sliced peeled fresh peaches
1 cup sugar
1/2 cup (1 stick) butter or margarine
3/4 cup all-purpose flour
2 teaspoons baking powder
1/8 teaspoon salt
1 cup sugar
3/4 cup milk

Toss the peaches with 1 cup sugar in a bowl. Melt the butter in an 8x8-inch baking dish. Sift the flour, baking powder and salt into a bowl and mix well. Stir in 1 cup sugar. Add the milk gradually, stirring constantly until a batter forms.

Pour the batter into the prepared baking dish; do not stir. Spoon the peach mixture over the batter; do not stir. Bake at 350 degrees for 1 hour. Serve hot or chilled with cream, if desired.

Note: Decrease the amount of sugar if the peaches are sweet and juicy.

Yield: 6 servings

 Nutrients Per Serving: Cal 560; Cal from Fat 145; T Fat 16.2 g; Saturated Fat 10 g; 25.9% Cal from Fat; Chol 43 mg; Sod 340 mg; T Carbo 100.4 g; 71.7% Cal from Carbo; Fiber 1.9 g; Prot 3.3 g; 2.4% Cal from Prot

Peach Pinwheel

1 cup sugar
2 tablespoons quick-cooking tapioca
1/2 teaspoon cinnamon
1/4 teaspoon salt
4 cups sliced peaches
1 cup water
1 cup biscuit mix
1 tablespoon sugar
1/3 cup light cream
1/4 cup (1/2 stick) butter, softened
2 tablespoons sugar
1/4 teaspoon cinnamon

Combine 1 cup sugar, the tapioca, 1/2 teaspoon cinnamon and the salt in a bowl and mix well. Stir in the peaches and water. Spoon into a greased 9×13-inch baking dish.

Mix the biscuit mix and 1 tablespoon sugar in a bowl. Add the cream gradually, stirring constantly until a soft dough forms. Knead the dough ten times on a lightly floured surface. Lightly pat or roll into a 6×6-inch square, approximately 1/4 inch thick.

Spread the pastry square with the butter and sprinkle with 2 tablespoons sugar and 1/4 teaspoon cinnamon. Roll as for a jellyroll to enclose the filling.

Cut the roll into 1/2-inch pinwheels and arrange the pinwheels cut side down over the peach mixture. Bake at 425 degrees for 25 minutes. Serve warm.

Yield: 8 servings

Nutrients Per Serving: Cal 383; Cal from Fat 87; T Fat 9.7 g; Saturated Fat 5.2 g; 22.7% Cal from Fat; Chol 22 mg; Sod 327 mg; T Carbo 71.9 g; 75.1% Cal from Carbo; Fiber 2.4 g; Prot 2.1 g; 2.2% Cal from Prot

Light Banana Cake

Cake

1 (2-layer) package banana cake mix
1 (12-ounce) can diet lemon-lime soda
1 or 2 ripe bananas, mashed

Banana Icing

2 cups fat-free banana cream yogurt
1 (3-ounce) package sugar-free banana pudding mix
8 ounces fat-free whipped topping
1 ripe banana, mashed

To prepare the cake, combine the cake mix, soda and banana in a bowl and mix well. Spread the batter in a 9x13-inch cake pan. Bake as directed on the package. Cool in the pan on a wire rack.

To prepare the icing, combine the yogurt and pudding mix in a bowl and mix well. Fold in the whipped topping and banana. Spread over the cake. Chill, covered, until serving time.

Yield: 12 servings

Nutrients Per Serving: Cal 109; Cal from Fat 5; T Fat 0.6 g; Saturated Fat 0.2 g; 4.6% Cal from Fat; Chol 0 mg; Sod 181 mg; T Carbo 24.2 g; 88.8% Cal from Carbo; Fiber 0.8 g; Prot 1.8 g; 6.6% Cal from Prot

Blueberry Butter Cake

1³/4 cups sifted all-purpose flour
2 teaspoons baking powder
¹/2 teaspoon salt
¹/3 cup butter, softened
1 cup sugar
2 eggs
¹/2 teaspoon vanilla extract
¹/2 cup milk
1¹/2 cups blueberries

Mix the flour, baking powder and salt together. Cream the butter in a mixing bowl. Gradually add the sugar to the butter, beating constantly until light and fluffy. Beat the eggs in a mixing bowl until thickened and add to the sugar mixture. Beat until blended and stir in the vanilla.

Add the dry ingredients to the sugar mixture alternately with the milk, beating until blended after each addition. Fold in the blueberries. Spoon the batter into a 9×13-inch cake pan and bake at 375 degrees for 20 to 30 minutes or until the cake tests done. Cool in the pan on a wire rack.

Yield: 12 servings

Nutrients Per Serving: Cal 146; Cal from Fat 56; T Fat 6.2 g; Saturated Fat 3.6 g; 38.4% Cal from Fat; Chol 50 mg; Sod 247 mg; T Carbo 20.9 g; 57.3% Cal from Carbo; Fiber 0.5 g; Prot 1.6 g; 4.4% Cal from Prot

Chocolate Sheet Cake

Cake

1 cup (2 sticks) butter or
   margarine, melted
2 cups sugar
2 cups all-purpose flour
1 cup water
1 teaspoon baking soda
1/2 cup buttermilk
1 teaspoon vanilla extract
2 eggs, lightly beaten

1/4 cup baking cocoa
1 teaspoon cinnamon

Fudge Frosting

1 cup sugar
1/2 cup (1 stick) butter
1/4 cup baking cocoa
1/4 cup milk
2 teaspoons vanilla extract
1 cup chopped pecans

To prepare the cake, melt the butter in a saucepan and stir in the sugar, flour and water. Bring to a boil and boil until thickened. Dissolve the baking soda in the buttermilk in a bowl and stir in the vanilla. Add the eggs, baking cocoa and cinnamon and mix well. Stir into the flour mixture.

Pour the batter into a greased and floured 9×13-inch cake pan. Bake at 350 degrees for 35 minutes. Cool in the pan on a wire rack.

To prepare the frosting, combine the sugar, butter, baking cocoa, milk, vanilla and pecans in a saucepan. Bring to a boil and boil for 1 minute, stirring frequently. Beat until thickened, cooled and of a spreading consistency. Spread over the top of the cake. Let stand until set.

Yield: 12 servings

 Nutrients Per Serving: Cal 583; Cal from Fat 277; T Fat 30.7 g; Saturated Fat 15.6 g; 47.5% Cal from Fat; Chol 97 mg; Sod 363 mg; T Carbo 71 g; 48.7% Cal from Carbo; Fiber 2.8 g; Prot 5.6 g; 3.8% Cal from Prot

Chocolate Chip Devil's Food Cake

Cake

1 (2-layer) package devil's food
   cake mix
1 (4-ounce) package chocolate
   instant pudding mix
4 eggs
1 1/4 cups brewed coffee, cooled
1/2 cup vegetable oil
1 tablespoon (heaping) baking cocoa
1 cup (6 ounces) chocolate chips

Cream Cheese Frosting

8 ounces cream cheese, softened
1 cup confectioners' sugar
1 tablespoon milk
1 teaspoon vanilla extract
Chocolate curls for garnish

To prepare the cake, combine the cake mix, pudding mix, eggs, coffee, oil and baking cocoa in a mixing bowl and beat for 2 minutes. Stir in the chocolate chips. Spoon the batter into a greased and floured 10-inch tube pan. Bake at 350 degrees for 50 to 60 minutes or until the cake tests done. Cool in the pan for 10 minutes and invert onto a cake plate.

To prepare the frosting, combine the cream cheese, confectioners' sugar, milk and vanilla in a mixing bowl and beat until of a spreading consistency. Spread the frosting over the top and partially down the side of the cake. Garnish with chocolate curls. Store, covered, in the refrigerator.

Yield: 12 servings

Nutrients Per Serving: Cal 382; Cal from Fat 217; T Fat 24.2 g; Saturated Fat 8.9 g; 56.8% Cal from Fat; Chol 91 mg; Sod 275 mg; T Carbo 37.1 g; 38.9% Cal from Carbo; Fiber 3.1 g; Prot 4.1 g; 4.3% Cal from Prot

> WHEN BAKING A CHOCOLATE OR DARK-COLORED CAKE,
> DUST THE PAN WITH BAKING COCOA IN LIEU OF FLOUR. IT WILL ELIMINATE
> THE WHITE FILM ON THE CAKE.

Chocolate Chip Applesauce Cake

2 cups all-purpose flour
2 tablespoons (heaping) baking cocoa
1 1/2 teaspoons baking soda
1 teaspoon cinnamon
1/2 teaspoon salt
1 1/2 cups granulated sugar

1/2 cup vegetable oil
2 eggs
2 cups applesauce
1 cup (6 ounces) chocolate chips
2 tablespoons brown sugar

Mix the flour, baking cocoa, baking soda, cinnamon and salt in a bowl. Beat the granulated sugar, oil and eggs in a mixing bowl until creamy. Add the flour mixture and beat until blended.

Spoon the batter into a greased 9×13-inch cake pan and sprinkle with the chocolate chips and brown sugar. Bake at 350 degrees for 40 to 45 minutes or until the cake tests done.

Yield: 12 servings

Nutrients Per Serving: Cal 348; Cal from Fat 144; T Fat 16 g; Saturated Fat 4.3 g; 41.4% Cal from Fat; Chol 35 mg; Sod 278 mg; T Carbo 49.5 g; 57% Cal from Carbo; Fiber 3.6 g; Prot 1.4 g; 1.6% Cal from Prot

FOR HEALTHIER CAKES, MUFFINS, AND BREADS, TRY
SUBSTITUTING UNSWEETENED APPLESAUCE FOR OIL WHEN BAKING.
USE THE SAME AMOUNT OF APPLESAUCE AS YOU WOULD OIL.

Carrot Cake

Cake
2¹/₂ cups all-purpose flour
2 teaspoons baking powder
1 teaspoon salt
1 teaspoon baking soda
2¹/₄ cups sugar
1¹/₂ cups vegetable oil
3 eggs
3 cups grated carrots

1 cup chopped pecans
2 teaspoons vanilla extract

Creamy Cream Cheese Frosting
8 ounces cream cheese, softened
¹/₂ cup (1 stick) butter, softened
2 teaspoons vanilla extract
1 (1-pound) package confectioners'
  sugar, sifted
1 cup chopped pecans

To prepare the cake, sift the flour, baking powder, salt and baking soda together. Beat the sugar, oil and eggs in a mixing bowl until creamy. Add the dry ingredients and beat until blended. Fold in the carrots, pecans and vanilla.

Spoon the batter into a greased and floured 9×13-inch cake pan or three greased and floured 9-inch cake pans. Bake the 9×13-inch cake pan at 350 degrees for 50 to 55 minutes or the 9-inch cake pans for 30 to 35 minutes or until the cake tests done. Cool the 9×13-inch pan on a wire rack. If using 9-inch cake pans, cool the layers in the pans for 10 minutes and remove to a wire rack to cool completely.

To prepare the frosting, beat the cream cheese, butter and vanilla in a mixing bowl until creamy. Add the confectioners' sugar and beat until of a spreading consistency. Spread the frosting over the top of the cake and sprinkle with the pecans. Store, covered, in the refrigerator.

Yield: 12 servings

 Nutrients Per Serving: Cal 943; Cal from Fat 505; T Fat 56.2 g; Saturated Fat 13.9 g; 53.6% Cal from Fat; Chol 95 mg; Sod 544 mg; T Carbo 102.2 g; 43.4% Cal from Carbo; Fiber 2.9 g; Prot 7.2 g; 3.1% Cal from Prot

Carrot Cake with Pineapple and Pecans

Cake

2²/₃ cups all-purpose flour
4 teaspoons baking powder
2 teaspoons cinnamon
1 teaspoon salt
1/2 teaspoon baking soda
2 pounds carrots, finely grated
    (7 cups)
1 cup granulated sugar
1 cup (2 sticks) unsalted butter
1 cup packed light brown sugar
2/3 cup granulated sugar

5 eggs
1¹/₂ teaspoons vanilla extract
1 (20-ounce) can crushed
    pineapple, drained
3/4 cup chopped pecans, toasted

Cream Cheese Frosting

16 ounces cream cheese, softened
10 tablespoons unsalted
    butter, softened
2¹/₂ cups confectioners' sugar
2¹/₂ cups sour cream

To prepare the cake, whisk the flour, baking powder, cinnamon, salt and baking soda in a large bowl. Toss the carrots with 1 cup sugar in a colander. Set the colander over a large bowl and drain for 20 to 30 minutes or until 1 cup of liquid has collected. Discard the liquid. Melt the butter in a large skillet over medium-low heat. Cook for 8 to 10 minutes or until golden brown, stirring frequently. Pour into a large bowl and cool for 10 minutes. Whisk in the brown sugar and 2/3 cup granulated sugar. Add the eggs one at a time, whisking constantly until blended after each addition. Stir in the vanilla. Add the flour mixture and stir just until almost combined. Fold in the carrots, pineapple and pecans. Spoon the batter into two generously greased and floured 9-inch cake pans and smooth the tops with a rubber spatula. Place the pans on the center oven rack. Bake at 350 degrees for 40 to 50 minutes or until the layers feel firm when lightly touched in the centers and wooden picks inserted in the centers come out clean. Cool in the pans for 10 minutes. Run a knife around the edges of the pans and invert onto the rack to cool completely.

To prepare the frosting, beat the cream cheese and butter in a mixing bowl at low speed until smooth. Add the confectioners' sugar and sour cream and beat until of a spreading consistency. Spread the frosting between the layers and over the top and side of the cake. Store, covered, in the refrigerator.

Yield: 12 servings

Nutrients Per Serving: Cal 893; Cal from Fat 416; T Fat 46.2 g; Saturated Fat 25.3 g; 46.6% Cal from Fat; Chol 198 mg; Sod 742 mg; T Carbo 108.9 g; 48.8% Cal from Carbo; Fiber 4.1 g; Prot 10.3 g; 4.6% Cal from Prot

Five-Flavor Pound Cake

Cake
3 cups all-purpose flour
1/2 teaspoon baking powder
3 cups sugar
1 cup (2 sticks) butter, softened
1/2 cup shortening
5 eggs
1/2 teaspoon rum extract
1/2 teaspoon butter extract
1/2 teaspoon lemon extract
1/2 teaspoon vanilla extract

1/2 teaspoon coconut extract
1 cup milk

Five-Flavor Glaze
1 cup sugar
1/2 cup water
1/2 teaspoon rum extract
1/2 teaspoon butter extract
1/2 teaspoon lemon extract
1/2 teaspoon vanilla extract
1/2 teaspoon coconut extract

To prepare the cake, sift the flour and baking powder together. Beat the sugar, butter, shortening, eggs and flavorings in a mixing bowl until blended. Add the flour mixture alternately with the milk, mixing well after each addition.

Spoon the batter into a lightly greased and floured tube pan. Bake at 325 degrees for 1 1/2 hours. Or, spoon the batter into two lightly greased and floured loaf pans and bake for 1 1/4 hours. Cool in the pan or pans for 10 minutes and remove to a wire rack.

To prepare the glaze, combine the sugar, water and flavorings in a saucepan and bring to a boil. Boil until the sugar dissolves. Drizzle the warm glaze over the warm cake. Let stand until cool.

Yield: 16 servings

Nutrients Per Serving: Cal 476; Cal from Fat 181; T Fat 20 g; Saturated Fat 10.5 g; 38% Cal from Fat; Chol 102 mg; Sod 160 mg; T Carbo 68.8 g; 57.8% Cal from Carbo; Fiber 0.6 g; Prot 4.9 g; 4.1% Cal from Prot. Nutritional profile does not include rum extract, butter extract, lemon extract, or coconut extract.

Fresh Peach Cake

2 cups all-purpose flour
1 teaspoon baking soda
1/8 teaspoon salt
1 1/2 cups packed brown sugar
1/2 cup (1 stick) butter, softened

1 egg
1 cup buttermilk
4 peaches, peeled and chopped
1/4 cup granulated sugar
1 teaspoon cinnamon

Mix the flour, baking soda and salt together. Beat the brown sugar and butter in a mixing bowl until creamy. Add the egg and beat until blended. Add the flour mixture alternately with the buttermilk, beginning and ending with the flour mixture and mixing well after each addition. Fold in the peaches. Spread the batter in a greased 9×13-inch cake pan. Mix the granulated sugar and cinnamon in a bowl and sprinkle over the top. Bake at 350 degrees for 30 to 35 minutes or until the cake tests done. Serve warm.

Yield: 12 servings

Nutrients Per Serving: Cal 305; Cal from Fat 78; T Fat 8.6 g; Saturated Fat 5 g; 25.6% Cal from Fat; Chol 40 mg; Sod 245 mg; T Carbo 52.9 g; 69.4% Cal from Carbo; Fiber 1.4 g; Prot 3.8 g; 5% Cal from Prot

Rhubarb Upside-Down Cake

5 cups (1/2-inch) slices rhubarb
1 (3-ounce) package
    strawberry gelatin

1 cup sugar
3 cups miniature marshmallows
1 (2-layer) package yellow cake mix

Arrange the rhubarb over the bottom of a 9×13-inch glass baking dish. Do not use any other type of baking dish, as the rhubarb will turn it black. Sprinkle the gelatin and sugar over the rhubarb and top with the marshmallows. Prepare the cake mix using the package directions and spread over the prepared layers. Bake at 350 degrees for 50 to 60 minutes or until the cake tests done. Invert the cake onto a serving platter. Serve warm with whipped topping or ice cream.

Yield: 12 servings

Nutrients Per Serving: Cal 177; Cal from Fat 6; T Fat 0.7 g; Saturated Fat 0.2 g; 3.4% Cal from Fat; Chol 0 mg; Sod 74 mg; T Carbo 41.3 g; 93.2% Cal from Carbo; Fiber 0.9 g; Prot 1.5 g; 3.4% Cal from Prot

Rum Cake

Cake
1 (2-layer) package yellow cake mix
4 eggs
1 (4-ounce) package vanilla instant pudding mix
1/2 cup cold water
1/2 cup vegetable oil
1 cup chopped pecans

Rum Glaze
1/2 cup (1 stick) butter or margarine
1 cup sugar
1/4 cup water
1/2 cup rum

To prepare the cake, combine the cake mix, eggs, pudding mix, water and oil in a mixing bowl and beat until blended. Stir in the pecans. Spoon the batter into a greased bundt pan or tube pan. Bake at 350 degrees for 30 minutes or until a wooden pick inserted near the center comes out clean. Cool in the pan for 10 minutes and remove to a wire rack to cool.

To prepare the glaze, combine the butter, sugar and water in a saucepan and bring to a boil. Boil for 3 minutes and then stir in the rum. Drizzle the warm glaze over the cake. Let stand until cool.

Note: If the cake mix contains pudding mix, reduce the eggs to 3 and the oil to 1/3 cup.

Yield: 12 servings

Nutrients Per Serving: Cal 369; Cal from Fat 230; T Fat 25.6 g; Saturated Fat 7.2 g; 62.3% Cal from Fat; Chol 91 mg; Sod 266 mg; T Carbo 31.8 g; 34.5% Cal from Carbo; Fiber 0.6 g; Prot 3 g; 3.3% Cal from Prot

Sunshine Cake

Cake

1 (2-layer) package yellow cake mix
1 (16-ounce) can unsweetened applesauce
1 (11-ounce) can mandarin oranges in light syrup
4 egg whites
1 teaspoon vanilla extract

Pineapple Topping

1 (15-ounce) can crushed pineapple
8 ounces reduced-fat whipped topping
1 (3-ounce) package sugar-free vanilla instant pudding mix

To prepare the cake, combine the cake mix, applesauce, undrained mandarin oranges, egg whites and vanilla in a mixing bowl and mix well. Spread the batter in a 9×13-inch cake pan sprayed with nonstick cooking spray. Bake at 350 degrees for 35 to 40 minutes or until the cake tests done. Cool in the pan on a wire rack.

To prepare the topping, combine the undrained pineapple, whipped topping and pudding mix in a mixing bowl and beat until combined. Spread the topping over the cake. Store, covered, in the refrigerator.

Yield: 12 servings

Nutrients Per Serving: Cal 135; Cal from Fat 26; T Fat 2.9 g; Saturated Fat 2.3 g; 19.3% Cal from Fat; Chol 0 mg; Sod 69 mg; T Carbo 25.4 g; 75.4% Cal from Carbo; Fiber 1 g; Prot 1.8 g; 5.3% Cal from Prot

Hawaiian Wedding Cake

Cake
2 cups all-purpose flour
2 cups sugar
2 teaspoons baking soda
1 (20-ounce) can juice-pack crushed pineapple
2 eggs, lightly beaten
1 cup shredded coconut
1 cup chopped walnuts

Cream Cheese Frosting
8 ounces cream cheese, softened
1/2 cup (1 stick) margarine, softened
1 1/2 cups confectioners' sugar
2 teaspoons vanilla extract

To prepare the cake, mix the flour, sugar and baking soda in a bowl. Stir in the undrained pineapple and eggs. Mix in the coconut and walnuts. Spread the batter in a greased 9×13-inch cake pan. Bake at 350 degrees for 45 minutes or until the top is golden brown.

To prepare the frosting, beat the cream cheese and margarine in a bowl until creamy. Add the confectioners' sugar and vanilla and beat until of a spreading consistency. Spread the frosting over the warm cake. Let stand until cool. Store, covered, in the refrigerator.

Yield: 12 servings

 Nutrients Per Serving: Cal 543; Cal from Fat 207; T Fat 23.1 g; Saturated Fat 8 g; 38.1% Cal from Fat; Chol 56 mg; Sod 381 mg; T Carbo 76.5 g; 56.3% Cal from Carbo; Fiber 1.8 g; Prot 7.6 g; 5.6% Cal from Prot

Pumpkin Roll

Cake

1 cup sugar
3/4 cup all-purpose flour
1 teaspoon baking soda
1 teaspoon salt
1 teaspoon cinnamon
2/3 cup canned pumpkin
3 eggs, lightly beaten
Confectioners' sugar for sprinkling

Cream Cheese Filling and Assembly

8 ounces cream cheese, softened
2 tablespoons margarine, softened
1 cup confectioners' sugar
1 teaspoon vanilla extract

To prepare the cake, grease and flour a jelly roll pan. Line the bottom of the pan with waxed paper. Mix the sugar, flour, baking soda, salt and cinnamon in a bowl. Stir in the pumpkin and eggs and spread the batter in the prepared pan. Bake at 350 degrees for 20 minutes or until the cake springs back when lightly touched in the center.

Run a knife around the edges of the pan to loosen and turn the cake onto a tea towel sprinkled with confectioners' sugar. Peel off the waxed paper. Roll the cake tightly and freeze for 30 to 45 minutes.

To prepare the filling, beat the cream cheese and margarine in a mixing bowl until creamy. Add the confectioners' sugar and vanilla and beat until of a spreading consistency.

Unroll the cake roll and spread with the filling. Roll to enclose the filling and wrap in foil. Freeze until serving time. Thaw in the refrigerator before slicing.

Note: One 29-ounce can of pumpkin makes three cake rolls.

Yield: 10 servings

 Nutrients Per Serving: Cal 290; Cal from Fat 105; T Fat 11.8 g; Saturated Fat 5.9 g; 36.2% Cal from Fat; Chol 88 mg; Sod 514 mg; T Carbo 41.5 g; 57.2% Cal from Carbo; Fiber 0.9 g; Prot 4.8 g; 6.6% Cal from Prot

Chocolate Peanut Butter Fudge

Chocolate Fudge

3/4 cup (1 1/2 sticks) margarine
3 cups sugar
1 (5-ounce) can evaporated milk
2 cups (12 ounces) chocolate chips
1 (7-ounce) jar marshmallow creme
1 teaspoon vanilla extract

Peanut Butter Fudge

1 1/3 sticks margarine
3 cups sugar
1 (5-ounce) can evaporated milk
1 cup smooth peanut butter
1 (7-ounce) jar marshmallow creme
1 teaspoon vanilla extract

To prepare the chocolate fudge, melt the margarine in a saucepan over medium heat. Stir in the sugar and evaporated milk and bring to boil. Boil for 4 minutes. Remove from the heat and stir in the chocolate chips. Beat with a hand-held mixer until the chips melt and the mixture thickens. Add the marshmallow creme and vanilla and beat until smooth. Spread in a 9x13-inch dish coated with margarine.

To prepare the peanut butter fudge, melt the margarine in a saucepan over medium heat. Stir in the sugar and evaporated milk and bring to a boil. Boil for 4 minutes. Remove from the heat. Beat in the peanut butter, marshmallow creme and vanilla until blended using a hand-held mixer. Spread over the prepared layer. Chill, covered, in the refrigerator until firm. Cut into squares.

Note: Must use Parkay margarine and Carnation evaporated milk.

Yield: 54 squares

Nutrients Per Serving: Cal 231; Cal from Fat 101; T Fat 11.1 g; Saturated Fat 2.7 g; 43.7% Cal from Fat; Chol 2 mg; Sod 105 mg; T Carbo 30.9 g; 53.5% Cal from Carbo; Fiber 1.2 g; Prot 1.6 g; 2.8% Cal from Prot

Marbled Orange Fudge

1¹/₂ teaspoons butter
3 cups sugar
³/₄ cup whipping cream
³/₄ cup (1¹/₂ sticks) butter
1 (11-ounce) package white chocolate chips or vanilla chips
1 (7-ounce) jar marshmallow creme
1 tablespoon orange extract
12 drops of yellow food coloring
5 drops of red food coloring

Coat a 9×13-inch dish with 1¹/₂ teaspoons butter. Combine the sugar, cream and ³/₄ cup butter in a heavy saucepan. Cook over low heat until the sugar dissolves. Bring to a boil and boil for 4 minutes, stirring constantly. Remove from the heat and stir in the white chocolate chips and marshmallow creme until melted.

Reserve 1 cup of the marshmallow mixture. Stir the flavoring and food coloring into the remaining marshmallow mixture and spread in the prepared dish. Drop the reserved marshmallow mixture by tablespoonfuls over the top. Using a knife, cut through the mixture to swirl. Chill, covered, until firm. Cut into squares.

Note: Do not substitute margarine for the butter.

Yield: 54 squares

 Nutrients Per Serving: Cal 123; Cal from Fat 51; T Fat 5.7 g; Saturated Fat 4 g; 41.6% Cal from Fat; Chol 13 mg; Sod 38 mg; T Carbo 17.4 g; 56.8% Cal from Carbo; Fiber 0 g; Prot 0.5 g; 1.6% Cal from Prot

Tuxedo Brownies

1 (family-size) package fudge brownie mix
2 ounces white chocolate
2 tablespoons milk
8 ounces cream cheese, softened
$^1/_4$ cup confectioners' sugar
1 cup whipped topping
2 cups (12 ounces) semisweet chocolate chips, melted

Spray miniature muffin cups with nonstick cooking spray. Prepare the brownie mix using the package directions for cake-like brownies. Fill the prepared muffin cups two-thirds full. Bake at 325 degrees for 14 minutes or until the edges are set; do not overbake. Immediately press the tops of the brownies with a miniature wooden tart shaper to make indentations. Cool in the pan for 15 minutes. Remove the brownies to a wire rack to cool completely.

Combine the white chocolate and milk in a microwave-safe bowl. Microwave for 1 minute or until the chocolate melts. Beat the cream cheese and confectioners' sugar in a mixing bowl until creamy. Stir in the white chocolate mixture and fold in the whipped topping.

Pipe the cream cheese mixture evenly into the indentations. Drizzle with the semisweet chocolate. Arrange the brownies in an airtight container and chill for 1 to 3 hours.

Yield: 48 miniature brownies

Nutrients Per Serving: Cal 115; Cal from Fat 48; T Fat 5.4 g; Saturated Fat 2.5 g; 41.7% Cal from Fat; Chol 5 mg; Sod 50 mg; T Carbo 16 g; 55.6% Cal from Carbo; Fiber 1 g; Prot 0.8 g; 2.8% Cal from Prot

Cheesecake Bars

Pecan Crust
1 cup all-purpose flour
1/4 cup packed brown sugar
1/2 cup (1 stick) butter, melted
1 cup crushed pecans

Cream Cheese Filling
16 ounces cream cheese, softened
1 cup granulated sugar
3 eggs
1 teaspoon vanilla extract
2 tablespoons confectioners' sugar

To prepare the crust, mix the flour, brown sugar, butter and pecans in a bowl. Press over the bottom of a 9×9-inch baking pan. Bake at 350 degrees until light brown. Let stand until cool. Maintain the oven temperature.

To prepare the filling, beat the cream cheese, granulated sugar, eggs and vanilla in a mixing bowl until creamy. Spread over the baked layer and bake for 20 minutes. Cool in the pan on a wire rack. Sprinkle with confectioners' sugar and cut into bars. Store, covered, in the refrigerator.

Yield: 12 bars

Nutrients Per Serving: Cal 415; Cal from Fat 255; T Fat 28.3 g; Saturated Fat 14 g; 61.5% Cal from Fat; Chol 116 mg; Sod 208 mg; T Carbo 33.5 g; 32.3% Cal from Carbo; Fiber 1.2 g; Prot 6.4 g; 6.2% Cal from Prot

Frosted Pumpkin Bars

Bars

2 cups all-purpose flour
2 teaspoons cinnamon
1 teaspoon baking soda
1 teaspoon baking powder
1/2 teaspoon salt
1 cup canned pumpkin
1 cup vegetable oil
4 eggs, lightly beaten
1 cup chopped nuts (optional)

Cream Cheese Frosting

3 ounces cream cheese, softened
6 tablespoons margarine
1 1/2 cups confectioners' sugar
1 teaspoon vanilla extract
1 teaspoon milk

To prepare the bars, combine the flour, cinnamon, baking soda, baking powder and salt in a bowl and mix well. Mix the pumpkin, oil and eggs in a bowl until blended. Add the flour mixture and mix well. Stir in the nuts. Spread in a greased and floured 10×15-inch baking pan. Bake at 350 degrees for 20 to 25 minutes or until the bars test done. Cool in the pan on a wire rack.

To prepare the frosting, beat the cream cheese and margarine in a mixing bowl until creamy. Add the confectioners' sugar, vanilla and milk and beat until of a spreading consistency. Spread over the baked layer. Let stand until set and then cut into bars. Store, covered, in the refrigerator.

Yield: 36 bars

Nutrients Per Serving: Cal 135; Cal from Fat 84; T Fat 9.5 g; Saturated Fat 1.8 g; 62.1% Cal from Fat; Chol 26 mg; Sod 134 mg; T Carbo 11.1 g; 32.8% Cal from Carbo; Fiber 0.5 g; Prot 1.7 g; 5% Cal from Prot

Pumpkin Squares

Crust
1 (2-layer) yellow cake mix
1/2 cup (1 stick) butter or margarine, melted
1 egg, lightly beaten

Pumpkin Filling
1 (30-ounce) can pumpkin pie filling
2/3 cup milk
2 eggs, lightly beaten

Topping
1/4 cup sugar
1 teaspoon cinnamon
1/4 cup (1/2 stick) butter or margarine

To prepare the crust, grease the bottom of a 9×13-inch baking pan. Reserve 1 cup of the cake mix for the topping. Combine the remaining cake mix, the butter and egg in a bowl and mix well. Pat over the bottom of the prepared pan.

To prepare the filling, combine the pumpkin, milk and eggs in a bowl and mix until smooth. Spread the filling over the crust.

To prepare the topping, combine the reserved 1 cup cake mix, the sugar and cinnamon in a bowl and mix well. Cut in the butter until crumbly. Sprinkle over the top of the prepared layers and bake at 350 degrees for 45 to 55 degrees or until a knife inserted in the center comes out clean. Cool in the pan on a wire rack. Cut into squares.

Yield: 12 servings

Nutrients Per Serving: Cal 255; Cal from Fat 123; T Fat 13.7 g; Saturated Fat 8.1 g; 48.3% Cal from Fat; Chol 85 mg; Sod 334 mg; T Carbo 29.8 g; 46.8% Cal from Carbo; Fiber 6 g; Prot 3.1 g; 4.9% Cal from Prot

Idiot No-Bake Cookies

2 cups sugar
5 tablespoons baking cocoa
1/2 cup milk
1/2 cup (1 stick) margarine

1 cup peanut butter
1 teaspoon vanilla extract
3 cups quick-cooking oats

Mix the sugar and baking cocoa in a saucepan. Add the milk and margarine and bring to a boil. Boil for 1 minute, stirring frequently.

Remove from the heat and stir in the peanut butter and vanilla. Add the oats and mix well. Let stand until cool. Drop by teaspoonfuls onto a sheet of waxed paper. Let stand until firm. Store in an airtight container.

Yield: 36 cookies

Nutrients Per Serving: Cal 145; Cal from Fat 62; T Fat 6.8 g; Saturated Fat 1.3 g; 42.8% Cal from Fat; Chol 0 mg; Sod 65 mg; T Carbo 17.6 g; 48.6% Cal from Carbo; Fiber 1.3 g; Prot 3.1 g; 8.6% Cal from Prot

Monster Cookies

2 cups (4 sticks) butter, softened
2 pounds brown sugar
4 cups granulated sugar
12 eggs, lightly beaten
3 pounds peanut butter
18 cups rolled oats

1 (16-ounce) package "M & M's"
    Chocolate Candies
16 ounces chocolate chips
2 tablespoons plus 2 teaspoons
    baking soda
1 tablespoon light corn syrup

Cream the butter, brown sugar and granulated sugar in a large mixing bowl until light and fluffy. Stir in the eggs, peanut butter, oats, candies, chocolate chips, baking soda and corn syrup. Drop the dough by spoonfuls onto a cookie sheet. Bake at 350 degrees for 10 minutes. Cool on the cookie sheet for 2 minutes. Remove to a wire rack to cool completely. Store in an airtight container.

Yield: 300 cookies

Nutrients Per Serving: Cal 101; Cal from Fat 44; T Fat 4.8 g; Saturated Fat 1.9 g; 43.7% Cal from Fat; Chol 11 mg; Sod 70 mg; T Carbo 12 g; 47.6% Cal from Carbo; Fiber 1 g; Prot 2.2 g; 8.7% Cal from Prot

Soft Sugar Cookies

4 cups all-purpose flour
1 1/2 teaspoons baking soda
1/4 teaspoon cream of tartar
2 cups sugar
1 cup (2 sticks) butter, softened

1 cup buttermilk
3 eggs
2 teaspoons vanilla extract
3 tablespoons sugar

Mix the flour, baking soda and cream of tartar together. Combine 2 cups sugar, the butter, buttermilk, eggs and vanilla in a mixing bowl and beat until blended. Add the flour mixture and mix well. Drop the dough by teaspoonfuls onto a cookie sheet and sprinkle evenly with 3 tablespoons sugar. Bake at 400 degrees for 12 to 15 minutes or until light brown. Cool on the cookie sheet for 2 minutes. Remove to a wire rack to cool completely. Store in an airtight container.

Yield: 24 cookies

Nutrients Per Serving: Cal 226; Cal from Fat 77; T Fat 8.5 g; Saturated Fat 5 g; 34% Cal from Fat; Chol 47 mg; Sod 165 mg; T Carbo 34.2 g; 60.5% Cal from Carbo; Fiber 0.6 g; Prot 3.1 g; 5.5% Cal from Prot

Hershey Bar Pie

17 miniature marshmallows
1/2 cup (1 stick) butter
6 (1 1/2-ounce) Hershey candy bars
  with almonds, chopped

1 cup whipping cream
1 (9-inch) graham cracker pie shell
Whipped topping (optional)

Combine the marshmallows and butter in a double boiler and cook until blended, stirring frequently. Add the candy bars and cook until the candy bars melt. Remove from the heat and cool slightly. Stir in the cream.

Pour into the pie shell and chill, covered, in the refrigerator until set. Spread with whipped topping. Store, covered, in the refrigerator.

Yield: 8 servings

Nutrients Per Serving: Cal 430; Cal from Fat 286; T Fat 31.7 g; Saturated Fat 16.3 g; 66.5% Cal from Fat; Chol 54 mg; Sod 261 mg; T Carbo 31.8 g; 29.6% Cal from Carbo; Fiber 1.9 g; Prot 4.2 g; 3.9% Cal from Prot

Frozen Lemonade Pie

45 to 50 vanilla wafers, finely crushed
1/2 cup sugar
1/2 cup (1 stick) margarine, melted
12 ounces whipped topping

1 (6-ounce) can frozen lemonade
  concentrate
1 (14-ounce) can sweetened
  condensed milk

Combine the wafer crumbs, sugar and margarine in a bowl and mix well. Press two-thirds of the crumb mixture over the bottom and side of two 8-inch pie plates or over the bottom of a 9×13-inch dish.

Combine the whipped topping, lemonade concentrate and condensed milk in a bowl and mix well. Spoon evenly into the pie plates and sprinkle with the remaining wafer crumbs. Freeze, covered, until firm.

Yield: 16 servings

Nutrients Per Serving: Cal 312; Cal from Fat 136; T Fat 15.3 g; Saturated Fat 5.9 g; 43.5% Cal from Fat; Chol 8 mg; Sod 155 mg; T Carbo 42 g; 53.8% Cal from Carbo; Fiber 0 g; Prot 2.1 g; 2.7% Cal from Prot

Peanut Butter Pie

4 ounces cream cheese, softened
1/2 cup peanut butter
8 ounces whipped topping

3/4 cup confectioners' sugar
1 (9-inch) graham cracker pie shell

Combine the cream cheese and peanut butter in a mixing bowl and beat at low speed until light and fluffy. Add the whipped topping and confectioners' sugar gradually, beating constantly until blended. Spoon into the pie shell and freeze, covered, for 8 hours.

Yield: 8 servings

Nutrients Per Serving: Cal 333; Cal from Fat 210; T Fat 23.4 g; Saturated Fat 10.5 g; 63.1% Cal from Fat; Chol 16 mg; Sod 232 mg; T Carbo 24.5 g; 29.4% Cal from Carbo; Fiber 1 g; Prot 6.2 g; 7.5% Cal from Prot

Yogurt Pie

1 (3-ounce) package gelatin
  (flavor of choice)
1/4 cup boiling water

16 ounces fruit-flavor yogurt
  (use same flavor as gelatin)
8 ounces whipped topping
1 (9-inch) graham cracker pie shell

Dissolve the gelatin in the boiling water in a heatproof bowl. Add the yogurt and whipped topping and mix well.

Spoon into the pie shell. Chill, covered, in the refrigerator until cold. Serve immediately.

Yield: 8 servings

Nutrients Per Serving: Cal 276; Cal from Fat 98; T Fat 10.9 g; Saturated Fat 6.1 g; 35.5% Cal from Fat; Chol 3 mg; Sod 172 mg; T Carbo 40.5 g; 58.6% Cal from Carbo; Fiber 0 g; Prot 4.1 g; 5.9% Cal from Prot

Pecan Pie

Pastry
1 1/4 cups all-purpose flour
2 tablespoons confectioners' sugar
1/2 teaspoon salt
1/2 cup (1 stick) unsalted butter,
  chilled and cut into
  1/4-inch pieces
2 tablespoons shortening, frozen and
  cut into small pieces
1 egg white, chilled and lightly beaten
1 egg yolk, beaten

Pie
6 tablespoons unsalted butter, cut
  into 1-inch pieces
1 cup packed dark brown sugar
1/2 teaspoon salt
3 eggs
3/4 cup light corn syrup
1 tablespoon vanilla extract
2 cups pecans, toasted and chopped
  into small pieces

To prepare the pastry, combine the flour, confectioners' sugar and salt in a food processor fitted with a steel blade. Scatter the butter and shortening over the flour mixture and pulse for 10 to 15 seconds or until crumbly. Pour the crumb mixture into a medium bowl.

Mix the egg white with enough ice water to measure $1/4$ cup. Sprinkle over the flour mixture with a rubber spatula, using a folding motion to mix. Press down on the dough with the broad side of the spatula until the dough adheres. Shape the dough into a ball and flatten the ball into a round 4 inches in diameter. Dust lightly with flour and wrap tightly with plastic wrap. Chill for 1 hour or for up to 2 days.

Roll the dough into a 13-inch round on a lightly floured surface. Fit the pastry into a 9-inch glass pie plate. Trim the edge, allowing a $1/2$-inch overhang. Tuck the overhang under so that the folded edge is flush with the rim of the pie plate; flute the edge. Chill for 1 hour or until firm. Prick the side and bottom of the pastry with a fork. Line with heavy-duty foil, pressing the foil firmly against the pastry and extending it over the fluted edge. Prick the foil with a fork and chill while the oven is preheating.

Arrange the pastry on the center oven rack and bake at 400 degrees for 15 minutes or until set, pressing once or twice with mitt-protected hands to flatten any puffing if needed. Remove the foil and bake for 10 minutes or until the bottom begins to color. Remove the pie shell from the oven and brush the side and bottom with the egg yolk. Bake for 1 minute longer. Reduce the oven temperature to 275 degrees.

To prepare the pie, place the pie shell on the center oven rack in the oven if not already warm. Place the butter in a heatproof bowl and arrange the bowl in a skillet of simmering water. Simmer until the butter melts. Remove the bowl from the simmering water and stir the brown sugar and salt into the melted butter with a wooden spoon. Beat in the eggs and then the corn syrup and vanilla. Return the bowl to the simmering water and cook until the mixture is shiny and warm to the touch and a candy thermometer registers 130 degrees. Remove from the heat and stir in the pecans.

Pou into the warm pie shell and bake for 50 to 60 minutes or until the center feels set but soft like gelatin when lightly touched. Cool on a wire rack for 4 hours or until completely cooled.

Yield: 8 servings

 Nutrients Per Serving: Cal 729; Cal from Fat 412; T Fat 45.6 g; Saturated Fat 16.3 g; 56.5% Cal from Fat; Chol 161 mg; Sod 376 mg; T Carbo 72.1 g; 39.6% Cal from Carbo; Fiber 2.3 g; Prot 7.2 g; 3.9% Cal from Prot

State Fair Apple Pie

Oat Crust
3/4 cup all-purpose flour
1 teaspoon cinnamon
1/2 teaspoon salt
1/2 teaspoon baking powder
1/3 cup butter
1/2 cup rolled oats (do not use
    quick-cooking oats)
3 tablespoons cold milk

Apple Filling
2 cups chopped peeled apples

1 cup sugar
2 eggs, beaten
1/4 teaspoon salt

Walnut Crumb Topping
2/3 cup rolled oats
3/4 cup packed brown sugar
1 teaspoon cinnamon
3 tablespoons butter
1/3 cup chopped walnuts
1 teaspoon vanilla extract

To prepare the crust, mix the flour, cinnamon, salt and baking powder in a bowl. Cut in the butter until crumbly. Stir in the oats and milk. Press over the bottom and up the side of a 9-inch pie plate.

To prepare the filling, toss the apples with the sugar in a bowl. Stir in the eggs and salt. Spoon into the prepared pie plate.

To prepare the topping, combine the oats, brown sugar and cinnamon in a bowl. Cut in the butter until crumbly. Stir in the walnuts and vanilla. Sprinkle over the top of the pie and bake at 350 degrees for 45 minutes.

Yield: 8 servings

Nutrients Per Serving: Cal 452; Cal from Fat 156; T Fat 17.1 g; Saturated Fat 8.4 g; 34.5% Cal from Fat; Chol 86 mg; Sod 400 mg; T Carbo 67.7 g; 60% Cal from Carbo; Fiber 2.7 g; Prot 6.2 g; 5.5% Cal from Prot

Understanding Food Labels

Labeling laws in the United States require the labels on processed foods to include specific information. Thus, understanding the food label allows you to choose the kind of food you desire to eat. The food label will provide information about the amounts of saturated fat, trans fat, cholesterol, fiber, sugar and calories from fat. Below is a list of helpful hints to consider when making your selection.

1.   Most manufacturers/producers list ingredients in descending order of weight, not volume.
2.   **Reduced calorie** means that the product contains at least 25 percent fewer calories than the "regular" product, whereas **low calorie** means 40 or fewer calories per serving.
3.   **Reduced fat** means that the product contains at least 25 percent less fat than the regular product, whereas **low fat** means 3 grams or fewer of fat per serving. **Light** means 50 percent less fat than the regular product. Food low in fat may be high in sugar.
4.   **High fiber** means that there are at least 5 grams of fiber per serving, as well as 3 grams or fewer of fat per serving. Note the level of total fat.
5.   **Reduced sodium** means that there is at least 25 percent less sodium than the regular product.
6.   **Reduced sugar** means that there is at least 25 percent less sugar than the regular product. A **sugar-free** product contains less than 0.5 grams of sugar per serving.
7.   **Trans fat** is an unsaturated fat that will raise the LDL or "bad" cholesterol. It is recommended to limit trans fat intake as much as possible.
8.   **"% Daily Value"** is the amount or percent of the USDA recommended nutrients which the product provides.

Contributors

Faith Anderson

Christine Barkdoll

Stacey Blizzard

Charlie Brown
(The Charles M. Schulz Family)

Susan Bussard

Fran Cordell

Caitlin Cremins

Karen Cremins

Sean Cremins

Thomas Cremins

Debby Cushwa

Jean Daywalt

Nina Dutrow

Tara Elwood

Pear Enam, MD

Donna Feightner

Sheila Ferreira

Alicia Foster

Nathaniel Fuller, MD

Lois Kretsch-Gemmill

Jean Gross

Annette Group

Jo Ann Gruber

Barbara Grumbine

Memoona Hanif

Robin Hoffman

Theresa Lang

Pam Lewis

Rebecca Makdad

Amanda Martz

Krista Myers

Regina Nevels

Penny Nicarry

Elizabeth Nicholas, MD

Sonnie Oberholzer-Tracy

Sue Powell

Jeff Schriver

Karen Stumbaugh

Juan Tayler, MD

Denise Tyssens

Stephanie Young

B.J. Zimmerman

Index

Index

Index

Great Intentions

A Collection of Recipes from the Endoscopy Center at Robinwood

To order, contact
Endoscopy Center at Robinwood
11110 Medical Campus Road, Suite 248
Hagerstown, Maryland 21742

Telephone: 240-313-9800
Fax: 240-313-9801
Web site: www.endoscopycenteratrobinwood.com